CASUAL TO CLASSIC
fashions to crochet

Contents

General Information

Many of the products used in this pattern book can be purchased from local craft, fabric and variety stores, or from the Annie's Attic Needlecraft Catalog *(see Customer Service information on page 63).*

W9-BVY-662

CASUAL TO CLASSIC

fashions to crochet

Whether it's an evening outfit or something to wear on a date in the park, you'll appreciate the versatile, timeless, elegance of each pattern designed for this book. A girl's best friend can be an interchangeable wardrobe. The beautiful styles featured in *Casual to Classic* are high on fashion yet simple in design. These 9 beautiful cardigans and jackets plus 3 easy skirts are sure to turn heads. You'll find a wide variety of sizes for each project in this book. Three of the jackets are sized from X-small up to 5X-large. The rest of the projects range from X-small to 2X-large. So, grab a crochet hook and start stitching!

Chevron Lattice Sweater

Design by Joy Prescott

SKILL LEVEL

EXPERIENCED

FINISHED SIZES

Instructions given fit 28–30-inch bust *(X-small)*; changes for 32–34-inch bust *(small)*, 36–38-inch bust *(medium)*, 40–42-inch bust *(large)*, 44–46-inch bust *(X-large)* and 48–50-inch bust *(2X-large)* are in [ ].

FINISHED GARMENT MEASUREMENTS

Bust: 32½ inches *(X-small)* [39 inches *(small)*, 45½ inches *(medium)*, 52 inches *(large)*, 58½ inches *(X-large)*, 65 inches *(2X-large)*]

MATERIALS

- Red Heart LusterSheen fine (sport) weight yarn (4 oz/335 yds/113g per skein):
  3 [4, 4, 4, 5, 5] skeins #0007 vanilla
- Size G/6/4mm crochet hook or size need to obtain gauge
- Tapestry needle
- Sewing needle
- Hook and eye closure
- Matching sewing thread

GAUGE

2 chevrons (peak to peak) = 6 inches; 6 rows = 4 inches

PATTERN NOTES

Chain-3 at beginning of double crochet row counts as first double crochet unless otherwise stated.
Chain-4 at beginning of double crochet row counts as first double crochet and chain-1 space unless otherwise stated.

SPECIAL STITCHES

Cluster (cl): Yo, insert hook in next st or ch, yo, pull lp through, yo, pull through 2 lps on hook, yo, sk next 3 sts or chs, insert hook in next st or ch, yo, pull lp through, yo, pull through 2 lps on hook, yo, pull through all 3 lps on hook.

Double treble crochet decrease (dtr dec): Yo 3 times, insert hook in next st, yo, pull lp through, [yo, pull through 2 lps on hook] 3 times, *yo 3 times, insert hook in next st, yo, pull lp through, [yo, pull through 2 lps on hook] 3 times, rep from * once, yo, pull through all 4 lps on hook.

PATTERN

Row 1: Ch number of times indicated in instructions, 2 dc in 4th ch from hook *(beg 3 sk chs count as first dc)*, *dc in each of next 7 chs, **cl** *(see Special Stitches)*, dc in each of next 7 chs**, (dc, ch 3, dc) in next ch, rep from * across, ending last rep at **, 3 dc in last ch, turn.

Row 2: Ch 4 *(see Pattern Notes)*, dc in first st, *[ch 1, sk next st or ch, dc in next st] 3 times, ch 1, sk next st, cl, [ch 1, sk next st, dc in next st] 3 times**, ch 1, sk next ch, (dc, ch 3, dc) in next ch, rep from * across, ending last rep at **, ch 1, sk next st, (dc, ch 1, dc) in last st, turn.
When beg row 2 at valley, ch 3, **dc dec** *(see Stitch Guide)* in next 2 sts, continue in Pattern.
When ending row 2 at valley, work Pattern across to last 4 sts, dc dec in first and 3rd sts of next 3 sts, dc in last st, turn.

Row 3: Ch 3 *(see Pattern Notes)*, 2 dc in first st, *dc in each of next 7 sts or chs, cl, dc in each of next 7 sts or chs**, (dc, ch 3, dc) in next ch, rep from * across, ending last rep at **, 3 dc in last st, turn.
When beg row 3 at valley, ch 3, dc dec in next 3 sts, continue in Pattern across.
When ending row 3 at valley, work in Pattern across to last 4 sts, dc dec in next 3 sts, dc in last st, turn.

INSTRUCTIONS

BACK

Row 1 (RS): Ch 104 [124, 144, 164, 184, 204], work row 1 of Pattern. *(84 [100, 116, 132, 148, 164] dc, 5 [6, 7, 8, 9, 10] cls, 4 [5, 6, 7, 8, 9] ch-3 sps)*
Rows 2–27 [2–29, 2–29, 2–29, 2–31, 2–31]: [Rep rows 2 and 3 of Pattern alternately] 13 [14, 14, 14, 15, 15] times. Fasten off at end of last row.
Row 28 [30, 30, 30, 32, 32]: Sk first 10 sts, join with sl st in next st, ch 2, sk next st, dc in next st, *[ch 1, sk next st, dc in next st] 3 times, ch 1, sk next ch, (dc, ch 3, dc) in next ch, ch 1, sk next ch, [dc in next st, ch 1, sk next st] 3 times**, cl, rep from * across to last 13 sts, ending last rep at **, dc dec in first and last of next 3 sts, turn, leaving last 10 sts unworked. *(81 [101, 121, 141, 161, 181] sts and chs)*

Row 29 [31, 31, 31, 33, 33]: Ch 2, sk next st or ch, dc in next st, *dc in each of next 7 sts or chs, (dc, ch 3, dc) in next ch, dc in each of next 7 sts or chs**, cl, rep from * across, ending last rep at **, dc dec in next 2 dc, turn.

Row 30 [32, 32, 32 34, 34]: Ch 2, sk next st, dc in next st, *[ch 1, sk next st, dc in next st] 3 times, ch 1, sk next ch, (dc, ch 3, dc) in next ch, ch 1, sk next ch, [dc in next st, ch 1, sk next st] 3 times**, cl, rep from * across, ending last rep at **, dc dec in next 2 dc, turn.

Rows 31–34 [33–38, 33–38, 33–40, 35–42, 35–44]: [Rep rows 29 and 30 [31 and 32, 31 and 32, 31 and 32, 33 and 34, 33 and 34] alternately] 2 [3, 3, 4, 4, 5] times.

Row 35 [39, 39, 41, 43, 45]: Rep row 29.

Row 36 [40, 30, 42, 44, 46]: Ch 5, dtr in each of next 2 sts, tr in each of next 2 sts, dc in each of next 2 sts, hdc in each of next 2 sts, sk next ch, sl st in next ch, *sk next ch, hdc in each of next 2 sts, dc in each of next 2 sts, tr in each of next 2 sts, dtr in next st**, **dtr dec** *(see Special Stitches)* in next 3 sts, dtr in next st, tr in each of next 2 sts, dc in each of next 2 sts, hdc in each of next 2 sts, sk next ch, sl st in next ch, rep from * across ending last rep at **, dtr in each of last 2 dc, turn.

First Shoulder

Row 1: Ch 3, dc in each of next 9 [19, 29, 29, 39, 49] sts, leaving rem sts unworked, turn. *(10 [20, 30, 30, 40, 50] dc)*

Row 2: Ch 3, dc in each st across and in 3rd ch of beg ch-3, fasten off.

2nd Shoulder

Row 1: Join with sl st in first st on last row of Back, ch 3, dc in each of next 9 [19, 29, 29, 39, 49] sts, turn. *(10 [20, 30, 30, 40, 50] dc)*

Row 2: Ch 3, dc in each st across and in 3rd ch of beg ch-3, fasten off.

RIGHT FRONT

Row 1 (RS): Ch 24 [24, 44, 44, 64, 64], work row 1 of Pattern. *(21 [21, 41, 41, 61, 61] sts and chs)*

Row 2: Work row 2 of Pattern across to last st, (dc, ch 3, dc, ch 1, dc) in last st, turn. *(25 [25, 45, 45, 65, 65] sts and chs)*

Row 3: Ch 6, dc in 4th ch from hook *(beg 3 sk chs count as first dc)*, dc in each st and in each ch across to last dc before next cl, cl, dc in each st and in each ch across to beg ch-4, dc in next ch of beg ch-4, 2 dc in next ch of beg ch-4, turn. *(26 [26, 46, 46, 66, 66] sts and chs)*

Row 4: Work in Pattern across to last cl, cl, [ch 1, sk next st, dc in next st] across to last dc and beg 3 sk chs of beg ch-6, ch 1, sk next st, (dc, ch 3, dc, ch 1, dc) in 3rd ch of beg 3 sk chs of beg ch-6, turn. *(31 [31, 51, 51, 71, 71] sts and chs)*

Rows 5–10 [5–14, 5–10, 5–14, 5–10, 5–14]: [Rep rows 3 and 4 alternately] 3 [5, 3, 5, 3, 5] times. *(49 [61, 69, 81, 89, 101] sts and chs at end of last row)*

X-Small, Medium & X-Large Sizes Only

Row 11: Rep row 3. *(51 [71, 91] sts and chs)*

Row 12: Work row 2 of Pattern across to last 3 sts, dc dec in first and last of last 3 sts, turn.

Rows 13–21 [13–23, 13–25]: Work in Pattern.

Neck Shaping

Row 1: Work in Pattern across to last 7 sts, ch 1, sk next st, dc dec in first and last of next 3 sts, dc in next st, leaving rem sts unworked, turn. *(50 [70, 90] sts and chs)*

Row 2: Ch 3, sk next 2 sts, [dc dec in next 2 sts] twice, dc in each of next 2 sts, work in Pattern across, turn. *(48 [68, 88] sts and chs)*

Row 3: Work in Pattern across to last 7 sts and chs, ch 1, sk next st or ch, dc dec in first and last of next 3 sts, leaving rem sts unworked, turn. *(45 [65, 85] sts and chs)*

Row 4: Sl st in each of first 5 sts, ch 3, 2 dc in same st, work in Pattern across, turn. *(41 [61, 81] sts and chs)*

Row 5: Work in Pattern across to last 2 sts, ch 1, sk next st, dc in last st, turn. *(39 [59, 79] sts and chs)*

Row 6: Ch 3, [dc dec in next 2 sts or chs] twice, dc in next st, cl, work in Pattern across, fasten off. *(35 [55, 75] sts and chs)*

Armhole Shaping

Row 7: Join with sl st in 11th st, sk next st, dc in next st, work in Pattern across to last 2 sts, sk next st, dc in last st, turn. *(23 [43, 63] sts and chs)*

Row 8: Ch 3, sk next 2 sts or chs, dc dec in next 2 sts or chs, work in Pattern across to last 4 sts, dc dec in first and last of next 3 sts, dc in last st, turn. *(22 [42, 62] sts and chs)*

Row 9: Ch 3, dc dec in next 2 sts, work in Pattern across to last 3 sts, dc dec in first and last of last 3 sts, turn.

Row 10: Ch 3, [dc dec in next 2 sts or chs] twice, work in Pattern across to last 4 sts, [dc dec in next 2 sts] twice, turn. *(20 [40, 60] sts and chs)*

Row 11: Ch 3, dc dec in next 3 sts or chs, work in Pattern across to last 3 sts, dc dec in first and last of last 3 sts, turn.

Row 12: Ch 3, dc dec in first and last of next 3 sts, dc dec in next 2 sts, work in Pattern across to last 5 sts, dc dec in first and last of next 3 sts, dc dec in last 2 sts, turn. *(18 [38, 58] sts and chs)*

Row 13: Ch 3, dc dec in next 2 sts, work in Pattern across to last 7 sts, ch 1, sk next st, dc dec in first and last of next 3 sts, leaving rem sts unworked, turn. *(16 [36, 56] sts and chs)*

Row 14: Ch 3, sk next 2 sts, dc dec in next 2 sts, work in Pattern across to last 2 sts, dc dec in last 2 sts, turn.

Medium Size Only

Row [15]: Work in Pattern across to last peak, leaving rem sts unworked turn.

Row [16]: Work in Pattern across.

Row [17]: Work in Pattern across to last 8 sts, ch 1, sk next st, dc dec in first and last of next 3 sts, leaving rem sts unworked, turn.

Row [18]: Work in Pattern across, turn.

X-Large Size Only

Row [15]: Work in Pattern across to last peak, leaving rem sts unworked turn.

Row [16]: Ch 3, [dc dec in next 2 sts] twice, dc in next st, work in Pattern across, turn.

Row [17]: Work in Pattern across to last 8 sts, ch 1, sk next st, dc dec in first and last of next 3 sts, leaving rem sts unworked, turn.

Row [18]: Work in Pattern across, turn.

Small, Large & 2X-Large Sizes Only

Row [15]: Work row 3 of Pattern.

Rows [16–23, 16–23, 13–25]: Work in Pattern.

Neck Shaping

Row [1]: Work in Pattern across to last st, dc in last st, turn. *([59, 79, 99] sts and chs)*

Row [2]: Ch 3, dc in each of next 5 sts, work in Pattern across, turn. *([57, 77, 97] sts)*

Row [3]: Work in Pattern across to last 4 sts, [ch 1, sk next st, dc in next st] twice, turn. *([55, 75, 95] sts and chs)*

Row [4]: Ch 3, dc in next ch, cl, work in Pattern across, turn. *([53, 73, 93] sts and chs)*

Row [5]: Work in Pattern across to last 6 sts, ch 1, sk next st, cl, turn. *([51, 71, 91] sts and chs)*

Row [6]: Ch 3, [dc dec in next 2 sts or chs] twice, dc in each of next 5 sts or chs, work in Pattern across, turn, fasten off.

Armhole Shaping

Row [7]: Sk first 11 sts, join with sl st in next st, ch 4, sk next 3 sts, dc in next st, work in Pattern across to last 6 sts, ch 1, sk next st, dc in next st, ch 1, sk next st, dc dec in first and last of last 3 sts, turn.

Row [8]: Ch 3, sk next st, [dc dec in first and last of next 3 sts] twice, dc in next ch, (dc, ch 3, dc) in next st, work in Pattern across, turn. *([37, 57, 77] sts and chs)*

Row [9]: Work in Pattern across to last 6 sts, ch 1, sk next ch, dc dec in first and last of next 3 sts, dc in next st, leaving rem st unworked, turn. *([37, 57, 77] sts and chs)*

Row [10]: Sl st in each of first 4 sts, ch 3, dc in each of next 2 sts, work in Pattern across, turn. *([32, 52, 72] sts and chs)*

Row [11]: Ch 3, [dc dec in next 2 sts or chs] twice, dc in next st or ch, cl, work in Pattern across, turn. *([26, 46, 66] sts and chs)*

Row [12]: Ch 3, work in Pattern across to last 2 sts, ch 1, sk next st, dc in last st, turn. *([24, 44, 64] sts and chs)*

Row [13]: Ch 3, sk next 2 sts, dc dec in next 2 sts, work in Pattern across, turn. *([23, 43, 63] sts and chs)*

Rows [14 & 15]: Work in Pattern.

Large & 2X-Large Sizes Only

Row [16]: Work in Pattern across to last 6 sts, ch 1, sk next st, dc in next st, ch 1, sk next st, dc dec in first and last of last 3 sts, turn.

Row [17]: Ch 3, sk next st, [dc dec in next 2 sts] twice, dc in next st, work in Pattern across, turn.

Row [18]: Work in Pattern across to last 6 sts, ch 1, sk next st, [dc dec in first and last of next 3 sts] twice, leaving last st unworked, turn.

Row [19]: Sl st in each of first 5 sts, ch 3, work in Pattern across, turn.

Rows [20 & 21]: Work in Pattern across, turn.

All Sizes

Row 1: Adjusting for different sizes, rep row 36 of Back.

Shoulder Shaping

Row 2: Ch 3, dc in each of next 9 [19, 29, 29, 39, 49] sts and chs.

Row 3: Ch 3, dc in each st across, fasten off.

LEFT FRONT

Work same as Right Front reversing shaping.

SLEEVE

Make 2.

Row 1: Beg at cuff end, ch 64, work row 1 of Pattern. *(61 sts and chs)*

Row/Rows 2–4 [2–4, 2–4, 2–4, 2–4, 2]: Work in Pattern.

Row 5 [5, 5, 5, 5, 3]: Ch 5, dc in 4th ch from hook, dc in next ch, 3 dc in next st, work in Pattern across to last 2 sts, 3 dc in next st, 4 dc in last st, turn. *(67 sts and chs)*

Row 6 [6, 6, 6, 6, 4]: Ch 3, sk next 2 sts, (dc, ch 3, dc) in next st, work in Pattern across to last 4 sts, (dc, ch 3, dc) in next st, sk next 2 sts, dc in last st, turn. *(67 sts and chs)*

X-Small Size Only

Row 7: Ch 3, sk next 2 sts or chs, (dc, ch 3, dc) in next ch, work in Pattern across to last 4 sts and chs, (dc, ch 3, dc) in next ch, sk next 2 sts or sts, dc in last st, turn.

Rows 8 & 9: Rep rows 6 and 7.

Row 10: Ch 3, sk next 2 sts or chs, (dc, ch 3, dc) in next ch, work in Pattern across to last 3 sts, sk next 2 sts or chs, dc in last st, turn.

Row 11: Ch 3, dc in first st, dc in each of next 2 sts or chs, (dc, ch 3, dc) in next st or ch, work in Pattern across to last 4 sts and chs, (dc, ch 3, dc) in next ch, dc in each of next 2 chs or sts, 2 dc in last st, turn. *(73 sts and chs)*

Row 12: Ch 3, sk next st, dc in next st, work in Pattern across to last 4 sts, ch 1, sk next st, dc in next st, sk next st, dc in next st, turn. *(75 sts and chs)*

Row 13: Ch 3, sk next st, [dc dec in next 2 sts or chs] twice, dc in next ch, (dc, ch 3, dc) in next ch, work in Pattern across to last 7 sts, dc in next ch, [dc dec in next 2 sts] twice, sk next st, dc in last st, turn. *(73 sts and chs)*

Rows 14 & 15: Rep rows 12 and 13.

Row 16: Ch 3, sk next st, dc in next st, work in Pattern across to last 4 sts, ch 1, sk next st, dc in next st, sk next st, dc in last st, turn. *(75 sts and chs)*

Row 17: Ch 3, dc in each of next 6 sts and chs, (dc, ch 3, dc) in next st, work in Pattern across to last 7 sts, dc in each of last 7 sts, turn. *(79 sts and chs)*

Row 18: Ch 3, sk next 2 sts, dc in next st, work in Pattern across to last 3 sts, sk next 2 sts, dc in last st, turn.

Row 19: Ch 3, dc in each of next 8 sts and chs, (dc, ch 3, dc) in next ch, work in Pattern across to last 9 sts and chs, dc in each of last 9 sts and chs, turn. *(83 sts and chs)*

Rows 20–29: Work in Pattern. Fasten off at end of last row.

Small, Medium, Large & X-Large Sizes Only

Row [7]: Ch 3, sk next 2 sts or chs, (dc, ch 3, dc) in next ch, work in Pattern across to last 4 sts and chs, (dc, ch 3, dc) in next ch, sk next 2 sts or chs, dc in last st, turn.

Row [8]: Ch 3, sk next 2 sts or chs, (dc, ch 3, dc) in next ch, work in Pattern across to last 3 sts and chs, sk next 2 sts or chs, dc in last st, turn.

Row [9]: Ch 3, dc in first st, dc in each of next 2 sts or chs, (dc, ch 3, dc) in next st, work in Pattern across to last 4 sts and chs, (dc, ch 3, dc) in next ch, dc in each of next 2 sts and chs, 2 dc in last st, turn. *([73] sts and chs)*

Row [10]: Ch 3, sk next st, dc in next st, work in Pattern across to last 4 sts, ch 1, sk next st, dc in next st, sk next st, dc in last st, turn. *([75] sts and ch sps)*

Row [11]: Ch 3, sk next st, [dc dec in next 2 sts or chs] twice, dc in next ch, (dc, ch 3, dc) in next ch, work in Pattern across to last 7 sts and chs, dc in next st, [dc dec in next 2 sts or chs] twice, sk next st, dc in last st, turn. *([73] sts and chs)*

Row [12]: Ch 3, sk next st, dc in next st, work in Pattern across to last 4 sts, ch 1, sk next st, dc in next st, sk next st, dc in last st, turn. *([75] sts and chs)*

Row [13]: Ch 3, dc in each of next 6 sts and chs, (dc, ch 3, dc) in next st, work in Pattern across to last 7 sts, dc in each of last 7 sts, turn. *([79] sts)*

Row [14]: Ch 3, sk next 2 sts, dc in next st, work in Pattern across to last 3 sts, sk next 2 sts, dc in last st, turn.

Row [15]: Ch 3, [dc dec in next 2 sts or chs] twice, dc in each of next 4 sts, (dc, ch 3, dc) in next st, work in Pattern across to last 9 sts, dc in each of next 4 sts, [dc dec in next 2 sts or chs] twice, dc in last st, turn.

Row [16]: Ch 3, sk next 2 sts, dc in next st, work in Pattern across to last 3 sts, sk next 2 sts, dc in last st, turn. Drop lp from hook.

Note: Join separate strand of yarn with sl st in last st, ch 4, fasten off.

Row [17]: Pick up dropped lp, ch 7, dc in 4th ch from hook, cl, work in Pattern across to last 9 sts and chs, dc in each of next 7 sts and chs, cl, 2 dc in last ch, turn. *([85] sts and chs)*

Small & Medium Sizes Only

Row [18]: Ch 4, dc in first st, ch 1, cl, work in Pattern across to last st, ch 1, (dc, ch 1, dc) in last st, turn. *([89] sts and chs)*

Row [19]: Ch 3, dc in next st, ch 1, cl, work in Pattern across to last 2 sts, ch 1, dc in each of last 2 sts, turn. *([87] sts and chs)*

Row [20]: Ch 4, dc in first st, ch 1, cl, work in Pattern across to last st, ch 1, (dc, ch 1, dc) in last st, turn. *([89] sts and chs)*

Row [21]: Ch 5, dc in 4th ch from hook, dc in next ch, dc in each of next 2 sts or chs, cl, work in Pattern across to last 2 sts and chs, 2 dc in next st or ch, 3 dc in last st, turn. *([91] sts and chs)*

Row [22]: Ch 4, dc in same st, ch 1, dc in next st, ch 1, sk next st, cl, work in Pattern across to last 3 sts, ch 1, sk next st, dc in next st, ch 1, (dc, ch 1, dc) in last st, turn. *([94] sts and chs)*

Row [23]: Ch 3, dc in first st, dc in each of next 3 sts or chs, cl, work in Pattern across to last 4 sts or chs, dc in each of next 3 sts or chs, 2 dc in last st, turn. *([91] sts and chs)*

Row [24]: Ch 4, dc in same st, ch 1, dc in next st, ch 1, sk next st, cl, work in Pattern across to last 3 sts, ch 1, sk next st, dc in next st, ch 1, (dc, ch 1, dc) in last st, turn. *([93] sts and chs)*

Row [25]: Ch 5, 2 dc in 4th ch from hook, dc in next ch, dc in each of next 4 sts and chs, cl, work in Pattern across to last 4 sts and chs, dc in each of next 2 sts or chs, 3 dc in each of last 2 sts or chs, turn. *([97] sts or chs)*

Row [26]: Ch 4, dc in first st, [ch 1, sk next st, dc in next st] twice, ch 1, sk next st, cl, work in Pattern across to last 2 sts, ch 1, sk next st, (dc, ch 1, dc) in last st, turn.

Row [27]: Ch 3, 2 dc in first st, dc in each of next 5 sts and chs, cl, work in Pattern across to last 6 sts and chs, dc in each of next 5 sts, 3 dc in last st, turn.

Row [28]: Ch 4, dc in first st, [ch 1, sk next st, dc in next st] twice, ch 1, sk next st, cl, work in Pattern across to last 2 sts, ch 1, sk next st, (dc, ch 1, dc) in last st, turn, fasten off. *([101] sts and chs)*

2X-Large Size Only

Row [5]: Ch 3, dc in first st, dc in each of next 2 sts or chs, (dc, ch 3, dc) in next ch, work in Pattern across to last 3 sts and chs, dc in each of next 2 sts and chs, 2 dc in last st, turn. *([73] sts and chs)*

Row [6]: Ch 3, sk next st, dc in next st, work in Pattern across to last 4 sts, ch 1, sk next st, dc in next st, sk next st, dc in last st, turn. *([75] sts and chs)*

Row [7]: Ch 3, dc in each of next 6 sts and chs, (dc, ch 3, dc) in next ch, work in Pattern across to last 7 sts and chs, dc in each of last 7 sts and chs, turn. *([79] sts and chs)*

Row [8]: Ch 3, sk next 2 sts, dc in next st, work in Pattern across to last 3 sts, sk next 2 sts, dc in last st, turn. Drop lp from hook.

Note: Join separate strand of yarn with sl st in last st, ch 4, fasten off.

Row [9]: Pick up dropped lp, ch 7, dc in 4th ch from hook, cl, work in Pattern across to last 9 sts and chs, dc in each of next 7 sts and chs, cl, 2 dc in last ch, turn. *([85] sts and chs)*

Large, X-Large & 2X-Large Sizes Only

Row [18, 18, 10]: Ch 4, dc in 4th ch from hook, ch 1, starting at base of ch-4, cl, work in Pattern across, ch 1, (dc, ch 1, dc) in last st, turn. *([89] sts and chs)*

Row [19, 19, 11]: Ch 5, dc in 4th ch from hook, dc in next ch, dc in each of next 2 chs or sts, cl, work in Pattern across to last 2 sts or chs, 2 dc in next ch, 3 dc in last ch, turn. *([91] sts and chs)*

Row [20, 20, 12]: Ch 5, dc in same st, ch 1, dc in next st, ch 1, sk next st, cl, work in Pattern across to last 3 sts, ch 1, sk next, dc in next st, ch 1, (dc, ch 1, dc) in last st, turn. *([93] sts and chs)*

Row [21, 21, 13]: Ch 5, 2 dc in 4th ch from hook, dc in next ch, dc in each of next 4 sts and chs, cl, work in Pattern across to last 4 sts and chs, dc in each of next 2 sts or chs, 3 dc in each of last 2 sts or chs, turn. *([97] sts and chs)*

Row [22, 22, 14]: Ch 4, dc in same st, [ch 1, sk next st, dc in next st] twice, ch 1, sk next st, cl, work in Pattern across to last 2 sts, ch 1, sk next st, (dc, ch 1, dc) in last st, turn.

Row [23, 23, 15]: Ch 5, dc in 4th ch from hook, dc in next ch, dc in each of next 6 sts, cl, work in Pattern across to last 2 sts or chs, 3 dc in each of last 2 sts or chs, turn. *([101] sts and chs)*

Row [24, 24, 16]: Work in Pattern across.

Row [25, 25, 17]: Ch 5, dc in 4th ch from hook, dc in next ch, 3 dc in next st, work in Pattern across to last 2 sts, 3 dc in next st, 4 dc in last st, turn. *([107] sts and chs)*

Row [26, 26, 18]: Ch 3, sk next 2 sts, (dc, ch 3, dc) in next st, work in Pattern across to last 4 sts, (dc, ch 3, dc) in next st, sk next 2 sts, dc in last st, turn.

Rows [27–30, 27–30, 19–22]: Rep rows [5–8] of 2X-Large. *([119] sts and chs at end of last row)*

Large & X-Large Sizes Only

Rows [31 & 32]: Work in Pattern across. Fasten off at end of last row.

2X-Large Size Only

Rows [33–38]: Rep rows [10–15].
Rows [39 & 40]: Work in Pattern across. Fasten off at end of last row.

All Sizes

Row 1: Join with sl st in center ch of ch-3 group on first chevron peak on Sleeve, ch 4, work in Pattern across to 2nd ch of ch-3 on last chevron peak, turn.

Rows 2–5: Work in Pattern across, turn. Fasten off at end of last row.

Row 6: Work in starting ch on opposite side of row 1, join with sl st in first ch, ch 5, dtr in each of next 2 sts, tr in each of next 2 sts, dc in each of next 2 sts, hdc in each of next 2 sts, sk next ch, sl st in next ch, *[sk next ch, hdc in each of next 2 sts, dc in each of next 2 sts, tr in each of next 2 sts, dtr in next st**, dtr dec in next 3 sts, dtr in next st, tr in each of next 2 sts, dc in each of next 2 sts, hdc in each of next 2 sts, sk next ch, sl st in next ch, rep from * across ending

last rep at **, dc in each of last 2 sts. Fasten off.

ASSEMBLY

Sew shoulder seams. Matching center of last row on Sleeves to shoulder seams, sew Sleeves in place. Sew Sleeve and side seams.

TRIM

Row 1: Working across bottom edge of Fronts and Back, with WS facing, join with sc in center ch at tip of first peak on first Front, sc in same st, sk next ch, ***hdc dec** *(see Stitch Guide)* in next 2 sts, dc dec in next 2 sts, **tr dec** *(see Stitch Guide)* in next 2 sts, **dtr dec** *(see Special Stitches)* in next 2 sts, dtr in next st, dtr dec in next 2 sts, tr dec in next 2 sts, dc dec in next 2 sts, hdc dec in next 2 sts, sk next ch, 2 sc in next ch, sk 1 ch, rep from * across Back to opposite peak on other Front, turn.

Rnd 2: Now working in rnds, ch 1, sc evenly spaced around entire outer edge, ending in multiple of 6 sts, join with sl st in beg sc.

Rnd 3: Ch 1, sc in first st, sk next 2 sts, 5 dc in next st, sk next 2 sts, *sc in next st, sk next 2 sts, 5 dc in next st, sk next 2 sts, rep from * around, join with sl st in beg sc, fasten off.

SLEEVE TRIM

Working in last row on 1 Sleeve, join with sc in seam, sc in each st around, join with sl st in beg sc, fasten off. Rep on other Sleeve.

FINISHING

Sew hook and eye to front opening. •

Slit Stitch Jacket

Design by Joy Prescott

FINISHED SIZES

Instructions given fit 28–30-inch bust *(X-small)*; changes for 32–34-inch bust *(small)*, 36–38-inch *(medium)*, 40–42-inch bust *(large)*, 44–46-inch bust *(X-large)*, 48–50-inch bust *(2X-large)*, 52–54-inch bust *(3X-large)*, 56–58-inch bust *(4X-large)* and 60–62-inch bust *(5X-large)* are in [ ].

FINISHED GARMENT MEASUREMENTS

Bust: 31 inches *(X-small)* [36 inches *(small)*, 38 inches *(medium)*, 43⅓ inches *(large)*, 46 inches *(X-large)*, 51 inches *(2X-large)*, 53½ inches *(3X-large)*, 58 inches *(4X-large)*, 64 inches *(5X-large)*]

MATERIALS

- Red Heart LusterSheen fine (sport) weight yarn (4 oz/335 yds/113g per skein):
    4 [4, 4, 5, 5, 5, 6, 6, 6] skeins #0360 chocolate
    1 skein each #0332 tan and #0913 warm red
- Size F/5/3.75mm crochet hook or size needed to obtain gauge
- Tapestry needle
- Sewing needle
- 6 brown ⅝-inch buttons
- 1 spool each of brown and tan sewing thread

19 sts = 4 inches; 12 pattern rows = 4 inches

Chain-3 at beginning of double crochet row or round counts as first double crochet unless otherwise stated.

Row 1: Ch 1, sc in first st, [sk next 2 sts, (2 dc, sc) in next st] across, turn.

Row 2: Ch 3 *(see Pattern Note)*, dc in each st across, turn.

INSTRUCTIONS

BACK

Row 1 (RS): Beg at bottom, with chocolate, ch 75, [87, 93, 105, 111, 123, 129, 141, 153], dc in 4th ch from hook *(beg 3 sk chs count as first dc)*, dc in each ch across, turn. *(73 [85, 91, 103, 109, 121, 127, 139, 151] dc)*

Row 2: Ch 1, sc in first st, *sk next 2 sts, (2 dc, sc) in next st, rep from * across, turn. *(73 [85, 91, 103, 109, 121, 127, 139, 151] sts)*

Row 3: Ch 3 *(see Pattern Note)*, dc in each st across, turn. *(73 [85, 91, 103, 109, 121, 127, 139, 151] dc)*

Rows 4–40 [4–40, 4–40, 4–42, 4–42, 4–42, 4–44, 4–44, 4–46]: Work in Pattern.

Armhole Shaping

Row 1: Sl st in each of first 7 [7, 7, 10, 10, 10, 13, 13, 13] sts, ch 3, dc in each st across, leaving last 6 [6, 6, 9, 9, 9, 12, 12, 12] sts unworked, turn. *(61 [73, 79, 85, 91, 103, 103, 115, 127] sts)*

Rows 2–17 [2–19, 2–21, 2–21, 2–23, 2–25, 2–25, 2–27, 2–29]: Work in Pattern.

First Shoulder

Row 1: Ch 1, sc in first st, [sk next 2 sts, (2 dc, sc) in next st] 4 [4, 5, 5, 6, 6, 6, 7, 8] times, leaving rem sts unworked, turn. *(13 [13, 16, 16, 19, 19, 19, 22, 25] sts)*

Row 2: Ch 3, dc in each st across, turn.

Row 3: Ch 1, sc in first st, *sk next 2 sts, (2 dc, sc) in next st, rep from * across, fasten off.

2nd Shoulder

Row 1: Sk next 35 [47, 47, 53, 53, 65, 65, 71, 77] sts on last row of Underarm Shaping, join with sl st in next st, ch 3, dc in each st across, turn. *(13 [13, 16, 16, 19, 19, 19, 22, 25] dc)*

Rows 2 & 3: Rep rows 2 and 3 of First Shoulder.

LEFT FRONT

Row 1: With chocolate, ch 45 [51, 54, 60, 63, 69, 72, 78, 84], dc in 4th ch from hook *(beg 3 sk chs count as first dc)* and in each ch across, turn. *(43 [49, 52, 58, 61, 67, 70, 76, 82] dc)*

Row 2: Ch 1, sc in first st, *sk next 2 sts, (2 dc, sc) in next st, rep from *, across, turn. *(43 [49, 52, 58, 61, 67, 70, 76, 82] sts)*

Row 3: Ch 3, dc in each st across, turn. *(43 [49, 52, 58, 61, 67, 70, 76, 82] dc)*

Rows 4–40 [4–40, 4–40, 4–42, 4–42, 4–42, 4–44, 4–44, 4–46]: Work in Pattern.

Armhole Shaping

Row 1: Ch 3, dc in each st across, leaving last 6 [6, 6, 9, 9, 9, 12, 12, 12] sts unworked, turn. *(37 [43, 46, 49, 52, 58, 58, 64, 70] dc)*

Neckline Shaping

Row 2: Sl st in each of first 10 sts, ch 1, sc in same st as last sl st, *sk next 2 sts, (2 dc, sc) in next st, rep from * across, turn. *(28 [34, 37, 40, 43, 49, 49, 55, 61] sts)*

Row 3: Ch 3, dc in each st across, leaving rem 3 [3, 3, 3, 3, 3, 3, 6] sts unworked, turn. *(25 [31, 34, 37, 40, 46, 46, 52, 55] dc)*

Row 4: Sl st in each of first 4 [7, 7, 7, 7, 7, 7, 7, 7] sts, ch 1, sc in same st as last sl st, *sk next 2 sts, (2 dc, sc) in next st, rep from * across, turn. *(22 [25, 28, 31, 34, 40, 40, 46, 49] sts)*

Row 5: Ch 3, dc in each st across, leaving last 3 [3, 3, 3, 3, 3, 3, 6, 6] sts unworked, turn. *(19 [22, 25, 28, 31, 37, 37, 40, 43] dc)*

Row 6: Sl st in each of first 4 [4, 4, 4, 4, 7, 7, 7, 7] sts, ch 1, sc in same st as last sl st, *sk next 2 sts, (2 dc, sc) in next st, rep from * across, turn. *(16 [19, 22, 25, 28, 31, 31, 34, 37] sts)*

Row 7: Ch 3, dc in each st across leaving last 3 [3, 3, 3, 3, 3, 3, 3] sts unworked, turn. *(13 [16, 19, 22, 25, 28, 28, 31, 34] dc)*

Small, Medium, Large & X-Large Sizes Only

Row [8]: Sl st in each of first 4 [4, 7, 7] sts, ch 1, sc in same st as last sl st, *sk next 2 sts, (2 dc, sc) in next st, rep from * across, turn. *([13, 16, 16, 19] sts)*

Row [9]: Ch 3, dc in each st across, turn.

2X-Large & 3X-Large Sizes Only

Row [8]: Sl st in each of first 7 sts, ch 1, sc in same st as last sl st, *sk next

2 sts, (2 dc, sc) in next st, rep from * across, turn. ([22, 22] sts)

Row [9]: Ch 3, dc in each st across, leaving last 3 sts unworked, turn. ([19, 19] dc)

4X-Large & 5X-Large Sizes Only

Row [8]: Sl st in each of first 4 sts, ch 1, sc in same st as last sl st, *sk next 2 sts, (2 dc, sc) in next st, rep from * across, turn. ([28, 31] sts)

Row [9]: Ch 3, dc in each st across, leaving last 3 sts unworked, turn. ([25, 28] dc)

Row [10]: Sl st in each of first 4 sts, ch 1, sc in same st as last sl st, *sk next 2 sts, (2 dc, sc) in next st, rep from * across, turn. ([22, 25] sts)

Row [11]: Ch 3, dc in each st across, turn.

All Sizes

Row 8 [10, 10, 10, 10, 10, 12, 12]: Ch 1, sc in first st, *sk next 2 sts, (2 dc, sc) in next st, rep from * across, turn.

Row 9 [11, 11, 11, 11, 11, 11, 13, 13]: Ch 3, dc in each st across, turn.

Rows 10–14 [12–16, 12–16, 12–16, 12–16, 12–18, 12–18, 14–18, 14–18]: [Rep rows 8 and 9 [10 and 11, 10 and 11, 10 and 11, 10 and 11, 10 and 11, 12 and 13, 12 and 13] alternately] 3 [3, 3, 3, 3, 4, 4, 3, 3] times.

Row 15 [17, 17, 17, 17, 19, 19, 19, 19]: Rep row 8 [10, 10, 10, 10, 10, 12, 12] 0 [1, 1, 1, 1, 0, 0, 1, 1] time. Fasten off at end of last row.

RIGHT FRONT

Work same as Left Front reversing shaping.

SLEEVE

Make 2.

Row 1: Beg at top, with chocolate, ch

21 [21, 24, 24, 27, 27, 30, 30, 33], dc in 4th ch from hook (beg sk 3 chs count as first dc) and in each ch across, turn. (19 [19, 22, 22, 25, 25, 28, 28, 31] dc)

Row 2: Ch 4, sc in 2nd ch from hook, sk next 2 chs, (2 dc, sc) in first st, *sk next 2 sts, (2 dc, sc) in next st, rep from * across, turn. (22 [22, 25, 25, 28, 28, 31, 31, 34] sts)

Row 3: Ch 5, dc in 4th ch from hook, dc in next ch, dc in each st across, turn. (25 [25, 28, 28, 31, 31, 34, 34, 37] dc)

Rows 4–18 [4–20, 4–21, 4–23, 4–24, 4–27, 4–28, 4–30, 4–31]: [Rep rows 2 and 3 alternately] 8 [9, 9, 10, 11, 12, 13, 14, 14] times.

Row 19 [21, 22, 24, 25, 28, 29, 31, 32]: Rep row 2 0 [0, 1, 1, 0, 1, 0, 0, 1] time. (73 [79, 85, 91, 97, 106, 112, 118, 124] sts at end of row)

Rows 20–23 [22–25, 23–26, 25–28, 26–29, 29–32, 30–33, 32–35, 33–36]: Work in Pattern.

Row 24 [26, 27, 29, 30, 33, 34, 36, 37]: Sl st in each of first 4 sts, working first st in same st as last sl st, work in Pattern across, leaving last 3 sts unworked, turn. (67 [73, 79, 85, 91, 100, 106, 112, 118] sts)

Rows 25–31 [27–33, 28–34, 30–35, 31–36, 34–38, 35–39, 37–40, 38–41]: Work in Pattern.

Rows 32–47 [34–49, 35–50, 36–56, 37–57, 39–62, 40–63, 41–65, 42–66]: [Rep rows 24–31 [26–33, 27–34, 29–35, 30–36, 33–38, 34–39, 36–40, 37–41] consecutively] 2 [2, 2, 3, 3, 4, 4, 5, 5] times. (55 [61, 67, 67, 73, 76, 82, 82, 88] sts at end of last row)

Row 48 [50, 51, 57, 58, 63, 64, 66, 67]: Rep row 24 [26, 27, 39, 30, 33, 34, 36, 37]. (49 [55, 61, 61, 67, 70, 76, 76, 82] sts)

Next rows: Work Pattern for 3 [3, 3, 2, 2, 1, 1, 1, 1] row(s). Fasten off at end of last row.

ASSEMBLY

Sew shoulder seams. Matching center of first row on Sleeves to shoulder seams, sew Sleeves in place gathering slightly at top of shoulders. Sew Sleeve and side seams.

SLEEVE TRIM

Rnd 1: Working in last row of 1 Sleeve, join tan with sl st in first st, ch 3, dc in each st around, join in 3rd ch of beg ch-3. Fasten off. (49 [55, 61, 61, 67, 70, 76, 76, 82] dc)

Rnd 2: Join warm red with sl st in first st, ch 3, *dc in each of next 2 sts, 2 dc in next st, rep from * around, join in 3rd ch of beg ch-3. (65 [73, 81, 81, 89, 93, 101, 101, 109] dc)

Rnd 3: Ch 3, work 86 [96, 107, 118, 123, 134, 134, 144] dc evenly spaced around, join in 3rd ch of beg ch-3, fasten off. (87 [97, 108, 119, 124, 135, 135, 145] dc)

Rep on other Sleeve.

NECK TRIM

Row 1: Join tan with sl st in top left corner at neck edge, ch 3, *dc in each of next 5 sts or rows, **dc dec** (see Stitch Guide) in next 2 sts, rep from * across neck edge to top right corner, working dc in last few sts or rows, turn.

Row 2: Ch 3, *dc in each of next 4 dc, dc dec in next 2 dc, rep from * across, working dc in last few sts, turn, fasten off.

Row 3: Join warm red with sc in first st, sc in each dc across, fasten off.

LOWER TRIM

Row 1: With RS of Jacket facing, join tan in lower left-hand corner, ch 3, dc in each st across, turn, fasten off.

Row 2: Join warm red with sl st in first st, ch 3, *dc in each of next 2 sts, 2 dc in next st, rep from * across, working dc in last rem st or sts, turn.

Row 3: Ch 3, *dc in each of next 2 sts, 2 dc in next st], rep from * across, working dc in last rem st or sts, turn.

Row 4: Ch 3, dc in each st across, fasten off.

PLACKET

Row 1: With tan, ch 85 [85, 88, 91, 94, 94, 97, 101, 107], dc in 4th ch from hook and in each ch across, turn. *(83 [83, 86, 89, 92, 92, 95, 99, 105] dc)*

Rows 2 & 3: Ch 3, dc in each st across, turn. Fasten off at end of last row.

Row 4: Join warm red with sc in first st, sc in each st across, fasten off.

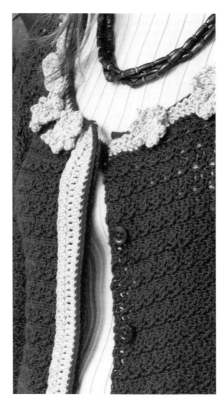

LARGE FLOWER
Make 2.

Rnd 1: With tan, ch 2, 6 sc in 2nd ch from hook, join with sl st in beg sc. *(6 sc)*

Rnd 2: Ch 1, (sc, ch 5, 2 tr, ch 3, sl st in top of last tr made, 2 tr, ch 5) in each st around, join with sl st in beg sc. Fasten off.

SMALL FLOWER
Make 2.

Rnd 1: With tan, ch 2, 6 sc in 2nd ch from hook, join in beg sc. *(6 sc)*

Rnd 2: Ch 1, (sc, ch 3, dc, ch 3, sl st in top of last dc made, dc, ch 3) in each st around, join in beg sc, fasten off.

LEAF
Make 2.

With tan, ch 10, sc in 2nd ch from hook, hdc in next ch, dc in each of next 2 chs, tr in next ch, dc in each of next 2 chs, hdc in next ch, 3 sc in last ch, working on opposite side of ch, hdc in next ch, dc in each of next 2 chs, tr in next ch, dc in each of next 2 chs, hdc in next ch, sc in last ch, join with sl st in beg sc, fasten off.

FINISHING

Place Placket down Right Front with sc even with edge of Front *(see photo)*, sew ends and long edge of tan section in place, leaving front sc unsewn.

Sew buttons evenly spaced down Left Front using sps between sts on Right Front as buttonholes.

Sew 1 Large Flower, 1 Small Flower and 1 Leaf to each side of Neck Trim as shown in photo. •

Crunch Stitch Jacket

Design by Joy Prescott

FINISHED SIZES

Instructions given fit 28–30-inch bust *(X-small)*; changes for 32–34-inch bust *(small)*, 36–38-inch bust *(medium)*, 40–42-inch bust *(large)*, 44–46-inch bust *(X-large)*, 48–50-inch bust *(2X-large)*, 52–54-inch bust *(3X-large)*, 56–58-inch bust *(4X-large)* and 60–62-inch bust *(5X-large)* are in [ ].

FINISHED GARMENT MEASUREMENT

Bust: 33 inches *(X-small)* [35 inches *(small)*, 39½ inches *(medium)*, 42²⁄₃ inches *(large)*, 47 inches *(X-large)*, 51 inches *(2X-large)*, 55 inches *(3X-large)*, 59¾ inches *(4X-large)*, 63 inches *(5X-large)*]

MATERIALS

- Lion Brand Microspun light (light worsted) weight yarn (2½ oz/168 yds/70g per ball):
  8 [9, 10, 10, 11, 11, 12, 13, 14] balls #102 blush
- Size G/6/4mm crochet hook or size needed to obtain gauge
- Tapestry needle

GAUGE

15 sts = 4 inches; 15 rows = 4 inches

PATTERN NOTES

Join with a slip stitch unless otherwise stated.

Chain-3 at beginning of double crochet row counts as first double crochet unless otherwise stated.

PATTERN

Row 1: Ch amount indicated in pattern, sc in 4th ch from hook *(beg 3 sk chs count as first dc)*, *dc in next ch, sc in next ch, rep from * across, turn.

Row 2: Ch 3 *(see Pattern Notes)*, sc in next st, *dc in next st, sc in next st, rep from * across, turn.

Rep row 2 for pattern.

INSTRUCTIONS

BACK

Row 1 (RS): Ch 64 [68, 76, 82, 90, 98, 106, 114, 120], work row 1 of Pattern. *(62 [66, 74, 80, 88, 96, 104, 112, 118] sts)*

Rows 2–41 [2–41, 2–44, 2–44, 2–48, 2–48, 2–51, 2–51, 2–51]: Work row 2 of Pattern.

Armhole Shaping

Row 42 [42, 45, 45, 49, 49, 53, 53, 53]: Sl st in each of first 7 [7, 7, 9, 9, 9, 11, 11, 13] sts, work row 2 of Pattern across, leaving last 6 [6, 6, 8, 8, 8, 10, 10, 12] sts unworked, turn. *(50 [54, 62, 64, 72, 80, 84, 92, 94] sts)*

Rows 43–64 [43–66, 46–69, 46–71, 50–75, 50–77, 54–81, 54–83, 54–83]: Work row 2 of Pattern.

First Shoulder

Row 1: Work row 2 of Pattern across first 16 [18, 20, 20, 24, 26, 26, 30, 30] sts, leaving rem sts unworked, turn. *(16 [18, 20, 20, 24, 26, 26, 30, 30] sts)*

Rows 2 & 3: Work row 2 of Pattern. Fasten off at end of last row.

2nd Shoulder

Row 1: Sk next 18 [18, 22, 24, 24, 28, 32, 32, 34] sts on last row of Back, join in next st, ch 3, sc in next st, *dc in next st, sc in next st, rep from * across, turn. *(16 [18, 20, 20, 24, 26, 26, 30, 30] sts)*

Rows 2 & 3: Work row 2 of Pattern. Fasten off at end of last row.

LEFT FRONT

Row 1: Ch 18 [20, 22, 26, 28, 30, 32, 36, 38], work row 1 of Pattern. *(16 [18, 20, 24, 26, 28, 30, 34, 36] sts)*

Row 2: Ch 1, (sc, dc) in first st, work in Pattern across, turn. *(17 [19, 21, 25, 27, 29, 31, 35, 37] sts)*

Row 3: Work in Pattern across to last st, (dc, sc) in last st, turn. *(18 [20, 22, 26, 28, 30, 32, 36, 38] sts)*

Rows 4–11 [4–13, 4–13, 4–13, 4–15, 4–15, 4–17, 4–17, 4–19]: [Rep rows 2 and 3 alternately] 4 [5, 5, 5, 6, 6, 7, 7, 8] times. *(26 [30, 32, 36, 40, 42, 46, 50, 54] sts at end of last row)*

Rows 12–41 [14–43, 14–44, 14–44, 16–48, 16–48, 18–51, 18–51, 20–53]: Work in Pattern.

Armhole Shaping
X-Small, Small, 3X-Large, 4X-Large & 5X-Large Sizes Only

Row 1: Work in Pattern across, leaving last 6 [6, 10, 10, 12] sts unworked, turn. *(20 [24, 36, 40, 42] sts)*

Row 2: Work in Pattern across to last 2 sts, **sc dec** *(see Stitch Guide)* in last 2 sts, turn. *(19 [23, 35, 39, 41] sts)*

Row 3: Ch 3 *(see Pattern Notes)*, sc dec in next 2 sts, work in Pattern across, turn. *(18 [22, 34, 38, 40] sts)*

Medium, Large, X-Large & 2X-Large Sizes Only

Row [1]: Sl st in each of first [6, 8, 8, 8] sts, work in Pattern across, turn. *([26, 28, 32, 34] sts)*

Row [2]: Ch 3, sc dec in next 2 sts, work in Pattern across, turn. *([25, 27, 31, 33] sts)*

Row [3]: Work in Pattern across to last 2 sts, sc dec in last 2 sts, turn. *([24, 26, 30, 32] sts)*

All Sizes

Rows 4–9 [4–7, 4–7, 4 & 5, 4 & 5, 4 & 5, 4 & 5, 4 & 5, 4 & 5]: Work in Pattern across.

Small & Medium Sizes Only

Rows [8 & 9]: Rep rows [2 and 3]. *([20, 22] sts)*

Rows [10 & 11]: Work in Pattern across.

Large, X-Large & 2X-Large Sizes Only

Rows [6 & 7]: Rep rows [2 and 3]. *([24, 28, 30] sts)*

Rows [8 & 9]: Work in Pattern across.

Rows [10–13]: Rep rows [6–9 consecutively]. *([22, 26, 28] sts)*

3X-Large & 4X-Large Sizes Only

Rows [6 & 7]: Rep rows [2 and 3]. *([32, 36] sts)*

Rows [8 & 9]: Work in Pattern across.

Rows [10–17]: [Rep rows 6–9 consecutively] twice. *([28, 32] sts at end of last row)*

Size 5X-Large Only

Rows [6 & 7]: Rep rows [2 and 3]. *([38] sts)*

Rows [8 & 9]: Work in Pattern across.

Rows [10–21]: [Rep rows 6–9 consecutively] 3 times. *([32] sts at end of last row)*

X-Small, Small, 3X-Large, 4X-Large & 5X-Large Sizes Only

Row 10 [12, 18, 18, 22]: Work in Pattern across to last 2 sts, sc dec in last 2 sts, turn. *(17 [19, 27, 31, 31] sts)*

Row 11 [13, 19, 19, 23]: Ch 3, sc dec in next 2 sts, work in Pattern across, turn. *(16 [18, 26, 30, 30] sts)*

Medium, Large, X-Large & 2X-Large Sizes Only

Row [12, 14, 14, 14]: Ch 3, sc dec in next 2 sts, work in Pattern across, turn. *([21, 21, 25, 27] sts)*

Row [13, 15, 15, 15]: Work in Pattern across to last 2 sts, sc dec in last 2 sts, turn. ([20, 20, 24, 26] sts)

All Sizes
Next rows: Work in Pattern for 14 [12, 12, 14, 15, 17, 13, 15, 12] rows. Fasten off at end of last row.

RIGHT FRONT
Row 1: Ch 18 [20, 22, 26, 28, 30, 32, 36, 38], work row 1 of Pattern. (16 [18, 20, 24, 26, 28, 30, 34, 36] sts)

Row 2: Ch 1, work in Pattern across to last st, (dc, sc) in last st, turn. (17 [19, 21, 25, 27, 29, 31, 35, 37] sts)

Row 3: Ch 1, (sc, dc) in first st, work in Pattern across, turn. (18 [20, 22, 26, 28, 30, 32, 36, 38] sts)

Rows 4–11 [4–13, 4–13, 4–13, 4–15, 4–15, 4–17, 4–17, 4–19]: [Rep rows 2 and 3 alternately] 4 [5, 5, 5, 6, 6, 7, 7, 8] times. (26 [30, 32, 36, 40, 42, 46, 50, 54] sts at end of last row)

Rows 12–41 [14–43, 14–44, 14–44, 16–48, 16–48, 18–51, 18–51, 20–53]: Work in Pattern.

Armhole Shaping
X-Small, Small, 3X-Large, 4X-Large & 5X-Large Sizes Only
Row 1: Sl st in each of first 6 [6, 10, 10, 12] sts, work in Pattern across, turn. (20 [24, 36, 40, 42] sts)

Row 2: Ch 3, sc dec in next 2 sts, work in Pattern across, turn. (19 [21, 35, 39, 41] sts)

Row 3: Work in Pattern across to last 2 sts, sc dec in last 2 sts, turn. (18 [22, 34, 38, 40] sts)

Medium, Large, X-Large & 2X-Large Sizes Only
Row [1]: Work in Pattern across to last 2 sts, sc dec in last 2 sts, turn. ([24, 26, 30, 32] sts)

Row [2]: Ch 3, sc dec in next 2 sts, work in Pattern across, turn. ([25, 27, 31, 33] sts)

All Sizes
Rows 3–8 [3–6, 3–6, 4 & 5, 3 & 4, 3 & 4, 3 & 4, 3 & 5]: Work in Pattern across.

Small, Medium, Large, X-Large, 2X-Large, 3X-Large, 4X-Large & 5X-Large Sizes Only
Next rows: Rep last 4 rows [1 1, 2, 2, 2, 3, 3, 4] times. ([16, 22, 22, 26, 28, 28, 32, 32] sts at end of last row)

Medium, Large, X-Large, 2X-Large Sizes Only
Next row: Work in Pattern across to last 2 sts, sc dec in last sts, turn. ([21, 21, 25, 27] sts)

Next row: Ch 3, sc dec in next 2 sts, work in Pattern across, turn. ([20, 20, 24, 26] sts)

X-Small, Small, 3X-Large, 4X-Large & 5X-Large Sizes Only
Next row: Ch 3, sc dec in next 2 sts, work in Pattern across to last 2 sts, sc dec in last 2 sts, turn. (17 [19, 27, 31, 31] sts)

Next row: Work in Pattern across to last 2 sts, sc dec in next 2 sts, turn. (16 [18, 26, 30, 30] sts)

All Sizes
Next rows: Work in Pattern for 14 [12, 12, 14, 15, 17, 13, 15, 12] rows. Fasten off at end of last row.

SLEEVE
Make 2.
Row 1: Beg at shoulder, ch 32 [32, 32, 36, 38, 40, 42, 46, 50], work row 1 of Pattern. (30 [30, 30, 34, 36, 38, 40, 44, 48] sts)

Row 2 (RS): Ch 1, (sc, dc) in first st, work in Pattern across to last sts, (sc, dc) in last st, turn. (32 [32, 32, 36, 38, 40, 42, 46, 50] sts)

Row 3: Ch 3, sc in same st, work in Pattern across to last st, (dc, sc) in last st, turn. (34 [34, 34, 38, 40, 42, 44, 48, 52] sts)

Rows 4–19 [4–21, 4–21, 4–23, 4–25, 4–25, 4–27, 4–27, 4–29]: [Rep rows 2 and 3 alternately] 8 [9, 9, 10, 11, 11, 12, 12, 13] times. (66 [70, 70, 78, 84, 86, 92, 96, 104] sts at end of last row)

Row 20 [22, 22, 24, 26, 26, 28, 28, 30]: Work in Pattern across.

X-Small, Small & Medium Sizes Only
Row 21 [23, 23]: Ch 1, sc dec in first 2 sts, work in Pattern across to last 2 sts, sc dec in last 2 sts, turn. (64 [68, 68] sts)

Rows 22 & 23 [24 & 25, 24 & 25]: Work in Pattern across.

Rows 24–61 [26–67, 26–67]: [Rep rows 21–23 consecutively] 13 [14, 14] times. (38 [40, 40] sts at end of last row)

Large, X-Large, 2X-Large, 3X-Large, 4X-Large & 5X-Large Sizes Only
Row [24, 26, 26, 28, 28, 30]: Ch 1, sc dec in first 2 sts, work in Pattern across to last 2 sts, sc dec in last 2 sts, turn. ([76, 82, 84, 90, 94, 102] sts)

Row [25, 27, 27, 29, 29, 31]: Work in Pattern across.

Rows [26–59, 28–65, 28–65, 30–73, 30–75, 32–85]: Rep rows [24 & 25, 26 & 27, 26 & 27, 28 & 29, 28 & 29, 30 & 31 alternately] [17, 19, 19, 23, 24, 27] times. ([42, 44, 46, 44, 46, 48] sts)

All Sizes

Next rows: Work in Pattern for 11 [9, 11, 19, 16, 19, 13, 12, 4] rows.

Trim

Row 1: Ch 3, dc in each st across, turn.

Rows 2 & 3: Ch 3, ***bpdc** *(see Stitch Guide)* around next st, **fpdc** *(see Stitch Guide)* around next st, rep from * across to last st, dc in last st, turn.

Row 4: Ch 1, sk first st, working left to right, **reverse sc** *(see Fig. 1)* in each st across. Fasten off.

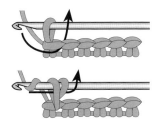

Reverse Single Crochet
Fig. 1

FINISHING

Sew shoulder seams. Matching center of first row on Sleeves to shoulder seams. Sew Sleeves in place. Sew Sleeve and side seams.

BODY TRIM

Rnd 1: Working around entire edge, evenly spacing sts, join in st at back of neck, ch 3, dc evenly spaced around edge, join in 3rd ch of beg ch-3.

Rnd 2: Ch 3, *bpdc around next st, fpdc around next st, rep from * around, join in 3rd ch of beg ch-3.

Rnd 3: Ch 3, *fpdc around next st, bpdc around next st, rep from * around, join in 3rd ch of beg ch-3.

Rnd 4: Ch 1, sk first st, reverse sc in each st around, join in beg sc, fasten off. •

Shell Stitch Cardigan

Design by Joy Prescott

EXPERIENCED

FINISHED SIZES

Instructions given fit 28–30-inch
bust *(X-small)*; changes for 32–34-
inch bust *(small)*, 36–38-inch bust
(medium), 40–42-inch bust *(large)*,
44–46-inch bust *(X-large)*, 48–50-
inch bust *(2X-large)* and 52–54-inch
bust *(3X-large)* are in [ ].

FINISHED GARMENT MEASUREMENTS

Bust: 29¾ inches *(X-small)* [35 inches
(small), 40¼ inches *(medium)*, 43¾
inches *(large)*, 49 inches *(X-large)*,
54¼ inches *(2X-large)*, 57¾ *(3X-
large)*]

MATERIALS

- Lion Brand Microspun
light (light worsted)
weight yarn (2½ oz/
168 yds/70g per ball):
7 [7, 8, 8, 9, 9, 10] balls #147 purple
- Size F/5/3.75mm and H/8/5mm
crochet hooks or size needed to
obtain gauge
- Tapestry needle
- Sewing needle
- Shank buttons:
  1-inch decorative: 1
  7/16-inch: 8
- Purple sewing thread

3 LIGHT

GAUGE

Size H hook: 2½ shells = 4 inches;
9 pattern rows = 4 inches

PATTERN NOTES

Chain-3 at beginning of double
crochet row counts as first double
crochet unless otherwise stated.

SPECIAL STITCHES

Shell: 5 dc in next st.
**Beginning half shell increase if
last row ended in single crochet
(beg half shell inc if last row
ended in sc):** Ch 4, sc in 2nd ch from
hook, sk next 2 chs, 5 dc in first sc.
**Beginning half-shell increase if
last row ended in double crochet
(beg half shell inc if last row
ended dc):** Ch 6, 2 dc in 4th ch from
hook, sk next 2 chs, sc in first dc.
**End half shell increase if row ends
with single crochet (end half
shell inc if row ends with sc):** (5
dc, sc) instead of 3 dc, in last 3.

PATTERN STITCHES

**Foundation row for odd number of
chains (foundation row for odd
number of chs):** Sc in 2nd ch from
hook, [sk next 2 chs, **shell** *(see
Special Stitches)* in next ch, sk next
2 chs, sc in next ch] across to last
3 chs, sk next 2 chs, 3 dc in last ch
(half shell), turn.
**Foundation row for even number of
chains (foundation row for even
number of chs):** Sc in 2nd ch from
hook, [sk next 2 chs, **shell** *(see
Special Stitches)* in next ch, sk next
2 chs, sc in next ch] across, turn.
**Beginning a row if last row ended
with a single crochet (Beg a row
if last row ended with a sc):** Ch 3,
2 dc in first st, work in Pattern across.

**Beginning a row in if last row ended
with double crochet (Beg a row if
last row ended with dc):** Ch 1, sc in
first st, work in Pattern across.
**Ending a row if last row ends with
single crochet (Ending a row if
last row ends with sc):** Work 3 dc
in last sc, turn.
**Ending a row if last row ends with
double crochet (Ending a row if
last row ends with dc):** Sc in last
st, turn.

INSTRUCTIONS

PATTERN

Work sc in center st of each shell and
shell in each sc.

BACK
Left Shoulder
Row 1: With size H hook, ch 17 [20,
23, 23, 26, 29, 29], work **foundation
row** *(see Pattern Stitches)*, turn.
Fasten off. *(2 [3, 3, 3, 4, 4, 4] shells,
1 [0, 1, 1, 0, 1, 1] half shell)*

Right Shoulder
Row 1: With size H hook, ch 17 [20,
23, 23, 26, 29, 29], work foundation
row, turn. *(2 [3, 3, 3, 4, 4, 4] shells,
1 [0, 1, 1, 0, 1, 1] half shell)*

Body
X-Small, Medium, Large, 2X-Large & 3X-Large Sizes Only
Row 2: Work in Pattern across, for
neckline, ch 14 [20, 20, 26, 26], sc
in first dc on Left Shoulder, work in

Pattern across, turn. *(4 [6, 6, 8, 8] shells, 2 [2, 2, 2, 2] half shells)*

Row 3: Work in Pattern across to last st, shell in last st, working across ch, sk first 2 chs, work in Pattern across to next Shoulder, sc in first dc of Shoulder, work in Pattern across, turn. *(7 [10, 10, 13, 13] shells, 1 [1, 1, 1, 1] half shell)*

Small & X-Large Sizes Only
Row [2]: Work in Pattern across, for **neckline**, ch [17, 23], 3 dc in first sc on Left Shoulder, work in Pattern across, turn. *([4, 6] shells, 4 half shells)*

Row [3]: Work in Pattern across sts and chs, turn. *([9, 12] shells)*

All Sizes
Work in Pattern for 11 [12, 13, 14, 15, 16, 17] rows.

Armhole Shaping X-Small & Medium Sizes Only
Rows 1 & 2: Beg half shell inc *(see Special Stitches)*, work in Pattern across, turn. *(8 [11] shells, 1 [1] half shell at end of last row)*

Small Size Only
Row [1]: Beg half shell inc, work in Pattern across, **end half shell inc** *(see Special Stitches)*, turn. *([10] shells)*

Large & 2X-Large Sizes Only
Row [1]: Ch 7, sc in 2nd ch from hook, sk next 2 chs, 5 dc in next ch, sk next 2 chs, sc in next dc, work in Pattern across to last st, drop yarn, with separate strand, join with sl st in last st, ch 6, fasten off, pick up dropped yarn, 5 dc in last st, sk next 2 chs, sc in next ch, sk next 2 chs, 3 dc in last ch, turn. *([12, 15] shells, [1] half shell)*

X-Large Size Only
Row [1]: Ch 7, sc in 2nd ch from hook, sk next 2 chs, 5 dc in next ch, sk next 2 chs, sc in next dc, work in Pattern across to last st, drop yarn, with separate strand, join with sl st in last st, ch 6, fasten off, pick up dropped yarn, sc in last st, sk next 2 chs, shell in next ch, sk next 2 chs, sc in last ch, turn. *([14] shells)*

3X-Large Size Only
Row [1]: Ch 12, 2 dc in 4th ch from hook, sk next 2 chs, sc in next ch, sk next 2 chs, 5 dc in next ch, sk next 2 chs, sc in next dc, work in Pattern across to last st, drop yarn, with separate strand, join with sl st in last st, ch 9, fasten off, pick up dropped yarn, 5 dc in last st, sk next 2 chs, sc in next ch, sk next 2 chs, 5 dc in next ch, sk next 2 chs, sc in last ch, turn. *([16] shells, [1] half shell)*

All Sizes
Work in Pattern until 37 [39, 41, 43, 45, 47, 49] rows are completed from Shoulders. Fasten off at end of last row.

LEFT FRONT
Row 1: Beg at shoulder, with size H hook, ch 14 [17, 20, 20, 23, 26, 26], work foundation row of Pattern, turn. *(2 [2, 3, 3, 3, 4, 4] shells, 0 [1, 0, 0, 1, 0, 0] half shell)*

X-Small Size Only
Rows 2–15: Work in Pattern across, working beg half shell inc at beg of rows 7, 14 and 15. *(3 shells, 1 half shell at end of last row)*

Small Size Only
Rows [2–17]: Work in Pattern across, working beg half shell inc at beg of rows [9], [16] and [17]. *([4] shells at end of last row)*

Medium Size Only
Rows [2–17]: Work in Pattern across, working beg half shell inc at beg of rows [7], [13], [16] and [17]. *([4] shells, [2] half shells at end of last row)*

Large Size Only
Rows [2–13]: Work in Pattern across, working beg half shell inc at beg of rows [7] and [13]. *([4] shells at end of last row)*

Rows [14–16]: Work in Pattern.

Row [17]: Ch 7, sc in 2nd ch from hook, sk next 2 chs, shell in next ch, sk next 2 chs, sc in next dc, work in Pattern across, turn. *([5] shells)*

Row [18]: Beg half shell inc, work in Pattern across, turn. *([5] shells, [1] half shell)*

X-Large Size Only
Rows [2–13]: Work in Pattern across, working beg half shell inc at beg of rows [7] and [13]. *([4] shells, [1] half shell)*

Rows [14–16]: Work in Pattern.

Row [17]: Ch 7, sc in 2nd ch from hook, sk next 2 chs, shell in next ch, sk next 2 chs, sc in next dc, work in Pattern across, turn. *([5] shells, [1] half shell)*

Row [18]: Beg half shell inc, work in Pattern across, turn. *([5] shells, [2] half shells at end of last row)*

2X-Large Size Only
Rows [2–17]: Work in Pattern across working beg half shell inc at beg of rows [5], [11] and [17]. *([5] shells, [1] half shell at end of last row)*

Row [18]: Work in Pattern.

Row [19]: Ch 9, 2 dc in 4th ch from hook, sk next 2 chs, sc in next ch, sk next 2 chs, 5 dc in next sc, work in

Pattern across, turn. *([6] shell, [1] half shell)*

Row [20]: Beg half shell inc, work in Pattern across, turn. *([7] shells)*

Row [21]: Beg half shell inc, work in Pattern across, turn. *([7] shells, [1] half shell)*

3X-Large Size Only

Rows [2–17]: Work in Pattern across working beg half shell inc at beg of rows [5], [11] and [17]. *([5] shells, [1] half shell)*

Row [18]: Work in Pattern across, turn.

Row [19]: Ch 10, sc in 2nd ch from hook, sk next 2 chs, shell in next ch, sk next 2 chs, sc in next ch, sk next 2 chs, shell in next sc, work in Pattern across, turn. *([7] shells)*

Row [20]: Beg half shell inc, work in Pattern across, turn. *([7] shells, [1] half shell)*

All Sizes

Next Rows: Work in Pattern for 13 [13, 13, 13, 14, 13, 15] rows.

Front Shaping
X-Small, Medium, Large & 2X-Large Sizes Only

Row 1: Work in Pattern across, leaving last 3 sts unworked, turn.

Row 2: Ch 1, sk first st, sl st in each of next 3 sts, work in Pattern across, turn.

Rows 3–6 [3–8, 3–8, 3–10]: [Rep rows 1 and 2 alternately] 2 [3, 3, 4] times. Fasten off at end of last row.

Small, X-Large & 3X-Large Sizes Only

Row [1]: Work in Pattern across, leaving last 3 sts unworked, turn.

Row [2]: Ch 1, sk first st, sl st in each of next 3 sts, work in Pattern across, turn.

Rows [3–6, 3–8, 3–10]: [Rep rows 1 and 2 alternately] [2, 3, 4] times.

Row [7, 9, 11]: Ch 1, sk next st, sl st in each of next 3 sts, work in Pattern across, turn, fasten off.

RIGHT FRONT
All Sizes

Row 1: Beg at shoulder, with size H hook, ch 14 [17, 20, 20, 23, 26, 26], work foundation row of Pattern, turn. *(2 [2, 3, 3, 4, 4] shells, 0 [1, 0, 0, 1, 0, 0] half shell)*

X-Small Size Only

Rows 2–15: Work in Pattern across, working beg half shell inc at beg of rows 6, 13 and 14. *(3 shells, 1 half shell at end of last row)*

Small Size Only

Rows [2–17]: Work in Pattern across, working beg half shell inc at beg of rows [8], [15] and [16]. *([4] shells at end of last row)*

Medium Size Only

Rows [2–17]: Work in Pattern across, working beg half shell inc at beg of rows [6], [12], [15] and [16]. *([4] shells, [2] half shells at end of last row)*

Large Size Only

Rows [2–13]: Work in Pattern across, working beg half shell inc at beg of rows [6] and [12]. *([4] shells at end of last row)*

Rows [14–16]: Work in Pattern.

Row [17]: Ch 7, sc in 2nd ch from hook, sk next 2 chs, shell in next ch, sk next 2 chs, sc in next dc, work in Pattern across, turn. *([5] shells)*

Row [18]: Beg half shell inc, work in Pattern across, turn. *([5] shells, [1] half shell)*

X-Large Size Only

Rows [2–13]: Work in Pattern across, working beg half shell inc at beg of rows [6] and [12]. *([4] shells, [1] half shell)*

Rows [14–16]: Work in Pattern.

Row [17]: Ch 7, sc in 2nd ch from hook, sk next 2 chs, shell in next ch, sk next 2 chs, sc in next dc, work in Pattern across, turn. *([5] shells, [1] half shell)*

Row [18]: Beg half shell inc, work in Pattern across, turn. *([5] shells, [2] half shells at end of last row)*

2X-Large Size Only

Rows [2–17]: Work in Pattern across working beg half shell inc at beg of rows [4], [10] and [16]. *([5] shells, [1] half shell at end of last row)*

Rows [18 & 19]: Work in Pattern.

Row [20]: Ch 7, sc in 2nd ch from hook, sk next 2 chs, shell in next sc, sk next 2 chs, sc in next ch, work in Pattern across, turn. *([6] shell, [1] half shell)*

Row [21]: Beg half shell inc, work in Pattern across, turn. *([7] shells)*

Row [22]: Beg half shell inc, work in Pattern across, turn. *([7] shells, [1] half shell)*

3X-Large Size Only

Rows [2–17]: Work in Pattern across working beg half shell inc at beg of rows [4], [10] and [16]. *([5] shells, [1] half shell)*

Rows [18 & 19]: Work in Pattern across, turn.

Row [20]: Ch 10, sc in 2nd ch from hook, sk next 2 chs, shell in next ch, sk next 2 chs, sc in next ch, sk next 2 chs, shell in next sc, work in Pattern across, turn. *([7] shells)*

Row [21]: Beg half shell inc, work in Pattern across, turn. *([7] shells, [1] half shell)*

All Sizes
Next Rows: Work in Pattern for 14 [14, 14, 14, 14, 14, 16] rows.

Front Shaping
X-Small, Medium, Large & 2X-Large Sizes Only
Row 1: Ch 1, sk first st, sl st in next 3 sts, work in Pattern across, leaving last 3 sts unworked, turn.
Row 2: Ch 1, work in Pattern across to last 3 sts, leaving last 3 sts unworked, turn.
Rows 3–6 [3–8, 3–8, 3–10]: [Rep rows 1 and 2 alternately] 2 [3, 3, 4] times. Fasten off at end of last row.

Small, X-Large & 3X-Large Sizes Only
Row [1]: Ch 1, sk first st, sl st in next 3 sts, work in Pattern across, leaving last 3 sts unworked, turn.
Row [2]: Ch 1, work in Pattern across to last 3 sts, leaving last 3 sts unworked, turn.
Rows [3–6, 3–8, 3–10]: [Rep rows 1 and 2 alternately] [2, 3, 4] times.
Row [7, 9, 11]: Ch 1, sk first st, sl st in each of next 3 sts, work in Pattern across, turn, fasten off.

SLEEVE
Make 2.
Row 1: With size H hook, ch 20 [20, 20, 23, 23, 26, 29], work in foundation row across, turn. *(3 [3, 3, 3, 3, 4, 4] shells, 0 [0, 0, 1, 1, 0,1] half shell)*
Rows 2–13 [2–14, 2–15, 2–17, 2–18, 2–19, 2–21]: Beg half shell inc, work in Pattern across, turn. *(9 [9, 10, 11, 12, 13, 14] shells, 0 [1, 0, 1, 0, 0, 1] half shell)*
Next rows: Work in Pattern for 33 [34, 34, 35, 35, 36, 36] rows.
Last row: Work in Pattern across, working **dc dec** *(see Stitch Guide)* in next 5 sts after each sc, unless 3-dc group follows a sc, fasten off.

CUFF
Make 2.
Row 1: With F hook, ch 19, sc in 2nd ch from hook and in each ch across, turn. *(18 sc)*
Rows 2–31 [2–31, 2–33, 2–34, 2–36, 2–38, 2–40]: Working in **back lps** *(see Stitch Guide)*, sc in each st across, turn.
Row 32 [32, 34, 35, 37, 39, 41]: For **buttonholes**, working this row in back lps, ch 1, sc in each of first 3 sts, [ch 1, sk next st, sc in each of next 3 sts] 3 times, ch 1, sk next st, sc in each of last 2 sts, turn. *(18 sts and chs)*
Row 33 [33, 35, 37, 40, 42]: Working in back lps, ch 1, sc in each st and ch across, turn, fasten off.

ASSEMBLY
Sew shoulder seams. Matching center of first row on Sleeve to shoulder seams, sew Sleeves in place. Sew Sleeve and side seams.
Stating at seam, sew Cuffs to Sleeves.
Sew 4 buttons to each Cuff opposite buttonholes.

LEFT FRONT TRIM
With size H hook, join with sc in upper front corner of Left Front, *sk next 2 rows, 9 dtr in next row, sk next 3 rows, sc in next row, rep from * across to dec rows at bottom of Left Front, **sk next 3 sts, 9 dtr in next st, sk next 3 sts, sc in next st, rep from ** across to Back, fasten off.

RIGHT FRONT TRIM
With size H hook, join with sc in first st of Right Front after Back, *sk next 3 sts, 9 dtr in next st, sk next 3 sts, sc in next st, rep from * across to ends of rows, **sk next 2 rows, 9 dtr in next row, sk next 3 rows, sc in next row, rep from ** across to top Front corner, fasten off.

FINISHING
Sew decorative button to Left Front as shown in photo. •

Leaf Green Sweater

Design by Joy Prescott

SKILL LEVEL

INTERMEDIATE

FINISHED SIZES

Instructions given fit 28–30-inch bust *(X-small)*; changes for 32–34-inch bust *(small)*, 36–38-inch bust *(medium)*, 40–42-inch bust *(large)*, 44–46-inch bust *(X-large)*, 48–50-inch bust *(2X-large)*, 52–54-inch bust *(3X-large)*, 56–58-inch bust *(4X-large)* and 60–62-inch bust *(5X-large)* are in [ ].

FINISHED GARMENT MEASUREMENTS

Bust: 32¾ inches *(X-small)* [36¾ inches *(small)*, 40¾ inches *(medium)*, 44¾ inches *(large)*, 48¾ inches *(X-large)*, 52¾ inches *(2X-large)*, 56¾ inches *(3X-large)*, 60¾ inches *(4X-large)*, 64¾ inches *(5X-large)*]

MATERIALS

- Red Heart Soft Yarn medium (worsted) weight yarn (5 oz/256 yds/140g per skein):
  4 [4, 5, 5, 5, 6, 6, 7, 7] skeins #9522 leaf
- Size I/9/5.5mm crochet hook or size needed to obtain gauge
- Tapestry needle
- Sewing needle
- ¾-inch decorative shank button
- Matching sewing thread

GAUGE

12 dc = 4 inches; 7 dc rows = 4 inches

PATTERN NOTES

Join with a slip stitch unless otherwise stated.

Chain-3 at beginning of double crochet row counts as first double crochet unless otherwise stated.

Chain-2 at beginning of half double crochet row counts as first double crochet unless otherwise stated.

SPECIAL STITCH

Shell: 5 dc in indicated stitch.

INSTRUCTIONS

BACK

Row 1 (RS): Ch 51 [57, 63, 69, 75, 81, 87, 93, 99], dc in 4th ch from hook *(beg 3 sk chs count as first dc)* and in each ch across, turn. *(49 [55, 61, 67, 73, 79, 85, 91, 97] dc)*

Rows 2–20 [2–20, 2–21, 2–21, 2–22, 2–22, 2–23, 2–23, 2–23]: Ch 3 *(see Pattern Notes)*, dc in each st across, turn.

Row 21 [21, 22, 22, 23, 23, 24, 24, 24]: For **underarm**, sl st in each of first 7 sts, ch 3, dc in each st across, leaving last 6 sts unworked, turn. *(37 [43, 49, 55, 61, 67, 73, 79, 85] dc)*

Rows 22–32 [22–32, 23–34, 23–34, 24–36, 24–36, 25–38, 25–38, 25–39]: Ch 3, dc in each st across, turn.

First Shoulder

Row 1: Ch 3, dc in each of next 11 [13, 15, 16, 18, 21, 23, 26, 28] sts, leaving rem sts unworked, turn. *(12 [14, 16, 17, 19, 22, 24, 27, 29] dc)*

Row 2: Ch 3, dc in each st across, turn. Fasten off.

2nd Shoulder

Row 1: Sk next 13 [15, 17, 21, 23, 23, 25, 25, 27] sts on last row of Back, join with sl st in next st, ch 3, dc in each rem st across, turn. *(12 [14, 16, 17, 19, 22, 24, 27, 29] dc)*

Row 2: Ch 3, dc in each st across, turn. Fasten off.

LEFT FRONT

Row 1: Ch 30 [33, 36, 39, 42, 45, 48, 51, 54], dc in 4th ch from hook *(beg 3 sk chs count as first dc)* and in each ch across, turn. *(28 [31, 34, 37, 40, 43, 46, 49, 52] dc)*

Rows 2–20 [2–20, 2–21, 2–21, 2–22, 2–22, 2–23, 2–23, 2–23]: Ch 3, dc in each st across, turn.

Armhole Shaping
X-Small & Small Sizes Only

Row 1: Sl st in each of first 7 sts, ch 3, dc in each st across to last 2 sts, **dc dec** *(see Stitch Guide)* in last 2 sts, turn. *(21 [24] dc)*

Row 2: Ch 3, dc dec in next 2 sts, dc in each rem st across, turn. *(20 [23] dc)*

Row 3: Ch 3, dc in each st across to last 2 sts, dc dec in last 2 sts, turn. *(19 [22] dc)*

Rows 4–11: [Rep rows 2 and 3 alternately] 4 times. *(11 [14] dc at end of last row)*

Rows 12–14 [12 & 13]: Ch 3, dc in each at across, turn. Fasten off at end of last row.

X-Large & 2X-Large Sizes Only

Row [1]: Sl st in each of first 7 sts, ch 3, dc in each st across to last 2 sts, dc dec in last 2 sts, turn. *([33, 36] dc)*

Row [2]: Ch 3, dc dec in next 2 sts, dc in each st across, turn. *([32, 35] dc)*

Row [3]: Ch 3, dc in each st across to last 2 sts, dc dec in last 2 sts, turn. *([31, 34] dc)*

Rows [4–15]: [Rep rows 2 and 3 alternately] [6] times. Fasten off at end of last row. *([19, 22] dc at end of last row)*

Medium Size Only

Row [1]: Ch 3, dc dec in next 2 sts, dc in each st across, leaving last 6 sts unworked, turn. *([27] dc)*

Row [2]: Ch 3, dc in each st across to last 2 sts, dc dec in last 2 sts, turn. *([26] dc)*

Row [3]: Ch 3, dc dec in next 2 sts, dc in each st across, turn. *([25] dc)*

Rows [4–13]: [Rep rows 2 and 3 alternately] [5] times. *([15] dc)*

Row [14]: Ch 3, dc in each st across, fasten off.

Large, 3X-Large & 4X-Large Sizes Only

Row [1]: Ch 3, dc dec in next 2 sts, dc in each st across, leaving last 6 sts unworked, turn. *([30, 39, 42] dc)*

Row [2]: Ch 3, dc in each st across to last 2 sts, dc dec in last 2 sts, turn. *([29, 38, 41] dc)*

Row [3]: Ch 3, dc dec in next 2 sts, dc in each st across, turn. *([28, 37, 40] dc)*

Rows [4–13, 4–15, 4–15]: [Rep rows 2 and 3 alternately] [5, 6, 6] times. *([18, 25, 28] dc)*

Row [14, 16, 16]: Dc in each st across to last 2 sts, dc dec in last 2 sts, fasten off.

5X-Large Size Only

Row [1]: Ch 3, at in next 2 sts, dc in each st across, leaving last 6 sts unworked, turn. *([45] dc)*

Row [2]: Ch 3, dc in each st across to last 2 sts, dc dec in last 2 sts, turn. *([44] dc)*

Row [3]: Ch 3, dc dec in next 2 sts, dc in each st across, turn. *([43] dc)*

Rows [4–17]: [Rep rows 2 and 3 alternately] [7] times. Fasten off at end of last row. *([29] dc)*

RIGHT FRONT

Work same as Left Front reversing shaping.

SLEEVE
Make 2.

Note: *For sizes Small, Medium, 4X-Large and 5X-Large, row 1 is RS of work; for sizes X-Small, Large, X-Large, 2X-Large and 3X-Large, row 2 is RS of work.*

Row 1: Ch 19 [21, 21, 21, 23, 23, 23, 23, 27], dc in 4th ch from hook *(beg 3 sk chs count as first dc)* and in each ch across, turn. *(17 [19, 19, 19, 21, 21, 21, 21, 25] dc)*

Rows 2–11 [2–13, 2–13, 2–13, 2–15, 2–15, 2–15, 2–15, 2–16]: Ch 3, dc in same st, dc in each st across to last st, 2 dc in last st, turn. *(37 [43, 43, 43, 49, 49, 49, 49, 55] dc at end of last row)*

Rows 12–15 [14–17, 14–17, 14–17, 16–19, 16–19, 16–19, 16–19, 17–20]: Ch 3, dc in each st across, turn.

Row 16 [18, 18, 18, 20, 20, 20, 20, 21]: Ch 3, dc dec in next 2 sts, dc in each st across to last 2 sts, dc dec in last 2 sts, turn. *(35 [41, 41, 41, 47, 47, 47, 47, 53] dc)*

Rows 17–26 [19–28, 19–28, 19–28, 21–30, 21–30, 21–30, 21–30, 22–31]: [Rep rows 12–16 [14–18, 14–18, 14–18, 16–20, 16–20, 16–20, 16–20, 17–21] consecutively] twice. *(31 [37, 37, 37, 43, 43, 43, 43, 49] dc at end of last row)*

Rows 27–29 [29–32, 29–32, 29–33, 31–35, 31–35, 31–35, 31–36, 32–37]: Ch 3, dc in each st across, turn.

Row 30 [33, 33, 34, 36, 36, 36, 37, 38]: Ch 1, sc in first st, *sk next 2 sts, **shell** *(see Special Stitch)* in next st, sk next 2 sts, sc in next st, rep from * across, turn. *[5 [6, 6, 6, 7, 7, 7, 7, 8] shells]*

Row 31 [34, 34, 35, 37, 37, 37, 38, 39]: Ch 3, 2 dc in same st, *sc in 3rd dc of next shell, shell in next sc, rep from * across to last shell, sc in 3rd dc of last shell, 3 dc in last st, turn. *(4 [5, 5, 5, 6, 6, 6, 6, 7] shells)*

Rows 32 & 33 [35 & 36, 35 & 36, 36 & 37, 38 & 39, 38 & 39, 38 & 39, 39 & 40, 40 & 41]: Rep last 2 rows once. Fasten off at end of last row.

ASSEMBLY

Sew shoulder seams. Matching center of first row on Sleeves to shoulder seams, sew Sleeves in place. Sew Sleeve and side seams.

BODY TRIM

Working around entire outer edge in sts and ends of rows, join with sc in side seam, evenly spacing sts around outer edge, sk next 2 sts, shell in next st, sk next 2 sts, *sc in next st/row, sk next 2 sts/rows, shell in next st/row, sk next 2 sts/rows, rep from * around, join in beg sc, fasten off.

FLOWER

Rnd 1: Ch 6, sl st in beg ch to form ring, ch 1, 12 sc in ring, join in beg sc. *(6 sc)*

Rnd 2: Ch 2 *(see Pattern Notes)*, (hdc, 3 dc, hdc) in **front lp** *(see Stitch Guide)* of each st around, join in 2nd ch of beg ch-2.

Rnd 3: Ch 1, working in **back lps** *(see Stitch Guide)* of rnd 1, (hdc, dc, 3 tr, dc, hdc) in each lp around, join in beg hdc, fasten off.

FINISHING

Sew Flower to Right Front over an opening between sts where neck shaping begins. Sew button to Left Front 2 inches from Front edge opposite Flower. Use sp between sts at center of Flower as buttonhole. •

Trellis Tunic

Design by Jill Hanratty

SKILL LEVEL

INTERMEDIATE

FINISHED SIZES

Instructions given fit 32–34-inch bust *(small)*; changes for 36–38-inch bust *(medium)*, 40–42-inch bust *(large)*, 44–46-inch bust *(X-large)*, 48–50-inch bust *(2X-large)*, 52–54-inch bust *(3X-large)* and 56–58-inch bust *(4X-large)* are in [ ].

FINISHED GARMENT MEASUREMENTS

Bust: 36 inches *(small)* [40 inches *(medium)*, 44 inches *(large)*, 48 inches *(X-large)*, 52 inches *(2X-large)*, 56 inches *(3X-large)*, 60 inches *(4X-large)*]

MATERIALS

- Red Heart LusterSheen fine (sport) weight yarn (4 oz/335 yds/113g per skein):
  5 [5, 6, 6, 7, 8, 9] skeins #0805 natural
  1 skein each #0360 chocolate and #0517 turquoise
- Size F/5/3.75mm crochet hook or size needed to obtain gauge
- Tapestry needle
- Stitch markers

GAUGE

2 ch sps and 1 shell = 2 inches; 7 pattern rows = 2 inches

PATTERN NOTES

Join with a slip stitch unless otherwise stated.

Chain-2 at beginning of a half double crochet row counts as first half double crochet unless otherwise stated.

SPECIAL STITCH
Shell: 5 dc in indicated st or ch sp.

INSTRUCTIONS

TUNIC
Waistband

Row 1: With chocolate, ch 4, (2 dc, ch 3, 3 dc) in 4th ch from hook *(beg 3 sk chs count as first dc)*, turn. *(6 dc, 1 ch-3 sp)*

Rows 2–63 [2–71, 2–79, 2–87, 2–95, 2–103, 2–111]: Ch 1, sl st in each of first 3 sts, sl st in next ch-3 sp, ch 3, (2 dc, ch 3, 3 dc) in same sp, turn.

Row 64 [72, 80, 88, 96, 104, 112]: Ch 1, sl st in each of first 3 sts, sl st in next ch-3 sp, ch 3, 2 dc in same sp, ch 1, sl st in starting ch on opposite side of row 1, ch 1, 3 dc in same ch. Fasten off.

BODICE

Rnd 1 (WS): Working in ends of rows, join turquoise with sc in end of first row, ch 3, *sc in end of next row, ch 3, rep from * around, join in beg sc, **turn.** Fasten off. *(64 [72, 80, 88, 96, 104, 112] ch sps)*

Rnd 2: Join natural in 2nd ch of first ch-3 sp, **ch 2** *(see Pattern Notes)*, 2 hdc in same ch, 3 hdc in 2nd ch of each ch-3 sp around, join in 2nd ch of beg ch-2, turn. Fasten off. *(64 [72, 88, 96, 104, 112] 3-hdc groups)*

Rnd 3: Working in sps between 3-hdc groups, join turquoise with sc in any sp, ch 3, *sc in next sp, ch 3, rep from * around, join in beg sc, turn. Fasten off.

Rnd 4: With chocolate, rep rnd 2.

Rnd 5: With turquoise, rep rnd 3.

Rnd 6: Rep rnd 2. **Do not fasten off.**

Rnd 7: Working in sps between 3-hdc groups, sl st in next sp, ch 1, sc in same sp, *ch 3, sc in 2nd hdc of next 3-hdc group, [ch 3, sc in next sp] 8 [9, 10, 11, 12, 13, 14] times, rep from * around to last 7 [8, 9, 10, 11, 12, 13] sps, ch 3, sc in 2nd hdc of next 3-hdc group, [ch 3, sc in next sp] 7 [8, 9, 10, 11, 12, 13] times, join in beg ch-1, dc in first sc *(counts as a ch-3 sp)*, turn. *(72 [80, 88, 96, 104, 112, 120] ch-3 sps)*

Rnd 8: Ch 1, sc in first ch-3 sp, **shell** *(see Special Stitch)* in next ch-3 sp, [sc in next ch-3 sp, ch 3] twice, *sc in next ch-3 sp, shell in next ch-3 sp**, [sc in next ch-3 sp, ch 3] twice, rep from * around, ending last rep at **, sc in next ch-3 sp, ch 3, sc in next ch-3 sp, join in beg ch-1, dc in first sc, turn. *(18 [20, 22, 24, 26, 28, 30] shells, 68 [76, 84, 92, 100, 108, 116] ch-3 sps)*

Rnd 9: Ch 1, sc in first ch-3 sp, *ch 3, sc in next ch-3 sp, ch 3, sc in next dc, ch 3, sk next 3 sts, sc in next st**, ch 3, sc in next ch-3 sp, rep from * around, ending last rep at **, join in beg ch-1, dc in first sc, turn. *(72 [80, 88, 96, 104, 112, 120] ch-3 sps)*

Rnd 10: Ch 1, sc in first ch-3 sp, *[ch 3, sc in next ch-3 sp] twice, shell in next ch-3 sp**, sc in next ch-3 sp, rep from * around, ending last rep at **, join in first sc, turn. *(18 [20, 22, 24, 26, 28, 30] shells, 36 [40, 44, 48, 52, 56, 60] ch-3 sps, 54 [60, 66, 72, 78, 84, 90] sc)*

Rnd 11: Sl st in next dc, ch 1, sc in same st, *ch 3, sk next 2 sts, sc in next st, [ch 3, sc in next ch-3 sp] twice**, ch 3, sc in next dc, rep from * around, ending last rep at **, join in

beg ch-1, dc in first sc, turn. *(72 [80, 88, 96, 104, 112, 120] ch-3 sps)*

Rnds 12–27: [Rep rnds 8–11 consecutively] 4 times.

BODICE BACK

Row 1: Now working in rows, ch 1, sc in first ch-3 sp, *shell in next ch-3 sp, sc in next ch-3 sp, [ch 3, sc in next ch sp] twice, rep from * 6 [7, 8, 8, 9, 9, 10] times, shell in next ch-3 sp, sc in next ch sp, leaving rem sts unworked, turn. *(8 [9, 10, 10, 11, 11, 12] shells, 14 [16, 18, 18, 20, 20] ch-3 sps)*

Row 2: Ch 1, sk first st, *sc in next dc**, ch 3, sk next 3 sts, sc in next st, [ch 3, sc in next ch-3 sp] twice, ch 3, rep from * across, ending last rep at **, ch 1, sk next 3 dc, dc in next dc, leaving last st unworked, turn. *(29 [33, 37, 37, 41, 41, 45] ch-3 sps)*

Row 3: Ch 3, sc in next ch-3 sp, *shell in next ch-3 sp, sc in next ch-3 sp**, [ch 3, sc in next ch-3 sp] twice, rep from * across, ending last rep at **, ch 1, dc in last ch-3 sp, turn. *(14 [16, 18, 18, 20, 20, 22] ch sps, 7 [8, 9, 9, 10, 10, 11] shells)*

Row 4: Ch 3, *sc in next dc, ch 3, sk next 3 sts, sc in next st**, [ch 3, sc in next ch-3 sp] twice, ch 3, rep from * across, ending last rep at **, ch 1, dc in 2nd ch of last ch-3 sp, turn. *(27 [31, 35, 35, 39, 39, 43] ch sps)*

Row 5: *[Ch 3, sc in next ch-3 sp] twice, shell in next ch-3 sp, sc in next ch-3 sp, rep from * across to last 2 ch-3 sps, ch 3, sc in next ch-3 sp, ch 1, dc in last ch-3 sp, turn. *(14 [16, 18, 18, 20, 20, 22] ch sps, 6 [7, 8, 8, 9, 9, 10] shells)*

Row 6: *Ch 3, sc in next ch-3 sp, ch 3, sc in next dc, ch 3, sk next 3 sts, sc in next dc, ch 3, sc in next ch-3 sp, rep from * across to last ch-3 sp, ch 1, dc in 2nd ch of last ch-3 sp, turn. (25 [29, 33, 33, 37, 37, 41] ch sps)

Row 7: Ch 3, 2 dc in same ch-3 sp, *sc in next ch-3 sp, [ch 3, sc in next ch-3 sp] twice**, shell in next ch-3 sp, rep from * across, ending last rep at **, 3 dc in 2nd ch of last ch-3, turn. (12 [14, 16, 16, 18, 18, 20] ch-3 sps, 5 [6, 7, 7, 8, 8, 9] shells, 2 3-dc groups)

Row 8: Ch 1, sc in first st, ch 3, sk next st, sc in next st, *[ch 3, sc in next ch-3 sp] twice, ch 3, sc in next dc**, ch 3, sk next 3 dc, sc in next dc, rep from * across, ending last rep at **, ch 1, dc in last st, turn. (25 [29, 33, 33, 37, 37, 41] ch sps)

Row 9: Ch 3, sc in first ch-3 sp, *ch 3, sc in next ch-3 sp, shell in next ch-3 sp, sc in next ch-3 sp, ch 3, sc in next ch-3 sp, rep from * across to last sc, ch 1, dc in last sc, turn. (14 [16, 18, 18, 20, 20, 22] ch sps, 6 [7, 8, 8, 9, 9, 10] shells)

Rows 10–21 [10–25, 10–25, 10–25, 10–25, 10–29, 10–29]: [Rep rows 6–9 consecutively] 3 [4, 4, 4, 4, 5, 5] times.

Row 22 [26, 26, 26, 26, 30, 30]: Rep row 6.

Right Back Shoulder
Small, Medium, Large & X-Large Sizes Only

Row 1 [1, 1, 1]: Ch 3, 2 dc in first ch sp, sc in next ch-3 sp, [ch 3, sc in next ch-3 sp] twice, shell in next ch-3 sp, sc in next ch-3 sp, ch 3, sc in next ch-3 sp, ch 1, dc in 2nd ch of next ch-3 sp (mark this ch), leaving rem sts unworked, turn. (4 ch-3 sps, 1 shell, 1 3-dc group)

2X-Large, 3X-Large & 4X-Large Sizes Only

Row [1, 1, 1]: Ch 3, 2 dc in first ch-3 sp, *sc in next ch-3 sp, [ch 3, sc in next ch-3 sp] twice, shell in next ch-3 sp, rep from * once, sc in next ch-3 sp, ch 3, sc in next ch-3 sp, ch 1, dc in 2nd ch of next ch-3 sp, leaving rem sts unworked, turn. ([6] ch-3 sps, [2] shells, [1] 3-dc group)

All Sizes

Row 2: Ch 1, sc in first ch sp, *ch 3, sc in next ch-3 sp, ch 3, sc in next dc, ch 3, sk next 3 dc, sc in next dc, ch 3, sc in next ch-3 sp, rep from * 0 [0, 0, 0, 1, 1, 1] time, ch 3, sc in next ch-3 sp, ch 3, sc in next dc, ch 1, dc in last st, turn. (7 [7, 7, 7, 11, 11, 11] ch sps)

Row 3: Ch 3, sc in first ch-3 sp, *ch 3, shell in next ch-3 sp**, sc in next ch-3 sp, ch 3, sc in next ch-3 sp, rep from * across, ending last rep at **, sc in last st, turn. (4 [4, 4, 4, 6, 6, 6] ch-3 sps, 2 [2, 2, 2, 3, 3, 3] shells)

Row 4: Ch 1, *sc in next dc, ch 3, sk next 3 sts, sc in next st**, [ch 3, sc in next ch-3 sp] twice, ch 3, rep from * across, ending last rep at **, ch 3, sc in next ch-3 sp, ch 1, dc in 2nd ch of last ch-3 sp, turn. (7 [7, 7, 7, 11, 11, 11] ch-3 sps)

Row 5: Ch 3, 2 dc in first ch-3 sp, [sc in next ch-3 sp, {ch 3, sc in next ch-3 sp} twice, shell in next ch-3 sp] 1 [1, 1, 1, 2, 2, 2] time(s), sc in next ch-3 sp, ch 3, sc in next ch-3 sp, ch 1, dc in last st, turn. (4 [4, 4, 4, 6, 6, 6] ch-3 sps, 1 [1, 1, 1, 2, 2, 2] shell(s), 1 3-dc group)

Row 6: Ch 1, sc in first dc, *ch 3, sc in next ch-3 sp, ch 3, sc in next dc**, ch 3, sk next 3 sts, sc in next dc, ch 3, sc in next ch-3 sp, rep from * across, ending last rep at **, ch 1, dc in 3rd ch of last ch-3, fasten off.

Left Back Shoulder

Row 1 (RS): Sk next 9 [13, 17, 17, 13, 13, 17] ch-3 sps on last row of Back, join in 2nd ch of next ch-3 sp, *[ch 3, sc in next ch-3 sp] twice**, shell in next ch-3 sp, sc in next ch-3 sp, rep from * across, ending last rep at **, 3 dc in 2nd ch of next ch-3 sp, turn. (4 [4, 4, 4, 6, 6, 6] ch-3 sps, 1 [1, 1, 1, 2, 2, 2] shell(s), 1 3-dc group)

Row 2: Ch 1, sc in first st, ch 3, sk next st, *sc in next st, [ch 3, sc in next ch-3 sp] twice**, ch 3, sc in next dc, ch 3, sk next 3 sts, rep from * across, ending last rep at **, turn. (7 [7, 7, 7, 11, 11, 11] ch sps)

Row 3: Ch 1, sc in first st, *shell in next ch-3 sp, sc in next ch-3 sp**, [ch 3, sc in next ch-3 sp] twice, rep from * across, ending last rep at **, ch 3, sc in next ch-3 sp, ch 1, dc in last st, turn. (4 [4, 4, 4, 6, 6, 6] ch sps, 2 [2, 2, 2, 3, 3, 3] shells)

Row 4: Ch 3, sc in next ch-3 sp, *ch 3, sc in next dc**, ch 3, sk next 3 dc, sc in next st, [ch 3, sc in next ch-3 sp] twice, rep from * across, ending last rep at **, ch 1, sk next 3 sts, dc in next st, leaving rem st unworked, turn. (7 [7, 7, 7, 11, 11, 11] ch-3 sps)

Row 5: Ch 1, sc in next ch-3 sp, *ch 3, sc in next ch-3 sp**, shell in next ch-3 sp, sc in next ch-3 sp, ch 3, sc in next ch-3 sp, rep from * across, ending last rep at **, 3 dc in 2nd ch of last ch-3 sp, turn. (3 [3, 3, 3, 5, 5, 5] ch-3 sps, 1 [1, 1, 1, 2, 2, 2] shell(s), 1 3-dc group)

Row 6: Ch 1, sc in first dc, ch 3, sk next dc, *sc in next dc**, [ch 3, sc in next ch-3 sp] twice, ch 3, sc in next dc, ch 3, sk next 3 dc, rep from * across, ending last rep at **, ch 3, sc in next ch-3 sp, ch 1, dc in last st, fasten off.

BODICE FRONT

Row 1: Sk next 5 [5, 5, 9, 9, 13, 13] unworked ch-3 sps on last row of

Bodice, join natural with sc in next ch-3 sp, *shell in next ch-3 sp, sc in next ch-3 sp, [ch 3, sc in next ch sp] twice, rep from * 6 [7, 8, 8, 9, 9, 10] times, shell in next ch-3 sp, sc in next ch-3 sp, leaving rem sts unworked, turn. *(8 [9, 10, 10, 11, 11, 12] shells)*

Row 2: Ch 1, sk first st, *sc in next dc**, ch 3, sk next 3 sts, sc in next st, [ch 3, sc in next ch-3 sp] twice, ch 3, rep from * across, ending last rep at **, ch 1, sk next 3 dc, dc in next dc, leaving last st unworked, turn. *(29 [33, 37, 37, 41, 41, 45] ch-3 sps)*

Row 3: Ch 3, sc in next ch-3 sp, *shell in next ch-3 sp, sc in next ch-3 sp**, [ch 3, sc in next ch-3 sp] twice, rep from * across, ending last rep at **, ch 1, dc in last ch-3 sp, turn. *(14 [16, 18, 18, 20, 20, 22] ch-3 sps, 7 [8, 9, 9, 10, 10, 11] shells)*

Row 4: Ch 3, *sc in next dc, ch 3, sk next 3 sts, sc in next st**, [ch 3, sc in next ch-3 sp] twice, ch 3, rep from * across, ending last rep at **, ch 1, dc in 2nd ch of last ch-3 sp, turn. *(27 [31, 35, 35, 39, 39, 43] ch sps)*

Row 5: *[Ch 3, sc in next ch-3 sp] twice, shell in next ch-3 sp, sc in next ch-3 sp, rep from * across to last 2 ch-3 sps, ch 3, sc in next ch-3 sp, ch 1, dc in last ch-3 sp, turn. *(14 [16, 18, 18, 20, 20, 22] ch-3 sps, 6 [7, 8, 8, 9, 9, 10] shells)*

Row 6: *Ch 3, sc in next ch-3 sp, ch 3, sc in next dc, ch 3, sk next 3 sts, sc in next dc, ch 3, sc in next ch-3 sp, rep from * across to last ch-3 sp, ch 1, dc in 2nd ch of last ch-3 sp, turn. *(25 [29, 33, 33, 37, 37, 41] ch-3 sps)*

Row 7: Ch 3, 2 dc in same ch-3 sp, *sc in next ch-3 sp, [ch 3, sc in next ch-3 sp] twice**, shell in next ch-3 sp, rep from * across, ending last rep at **, 3 dc in 2nd ch of last ch-3 sp, turn.

(12 [14, 16, 16, 18, 18, 20] ch-3 sps, 5 [6, 7, 7, 8, 8, 9] shells, 2 3-dc groups)

Row 8: Ch 1, sc in first st, ch 3, sk next st, sc in next st, *[ch 3, sc in next ch-3 sp] twice, ch 3, sc in next dc**, ch 3, sk next 3 dc, sc in next dc, rep from * across, ending last rep at **, ch 1, dc in last st, turn. *(25 [29, 33, 33, 37, 37, 41] ch sps)*

Row 9: Ch 3, sc in next ch-3 sp, *ch 3, sc in next ch-3 sp, shell in next ch-3 sp, sc in next ch-3 sp, ch 3, sc in next ch-3 sp, rep from * across to last sc, ch 1, dc in last sc, turn. *(14 [16, 18, 18, 20, 20, 22] ch sps, 6 [7, 8, 8, 9, 9, 10] shells)*

Rows 10–21 [10–25, 10–25, 10–25, 10–25, 10–29, 10–29]: [Rep rows 6–9 consecutively] 3 [4, 4, 4, 4, 5, 5] times.

Row 22 [26, 26, 26, 26, 30, 30]: Rep row 6.

Right Front Shoulder
Work same as Right Back Shoulder.

To join Right Shoulders, join natural with sl st in first st of 1 Shoulder on Front, ch 1, sl st in corresponding st on matching shoulder of Back, evenly spacing sts [ch 1, sl st in next st or ch-3 sp on Front, ch 1, sl st in next st or ch-3 sp on Back] across, fasten off.

Left Front Shoulder
Work same as Left Back Shoulder.

To join Left Shoulders, join natural with sl st in first st of 1 Shoulder on Front, ch 1, sl st in corresponding st on matching shoulder of Back, evenly spacing sts [ch 1, sl st in next st or ch-3 sp on Front, ch 1, sl st in next st or ch-3 sp on Back] across, fasten off.

NECK TRIM
Rnd 1: Working around neck opening, join natural in 1 shoulder seam, ch 2, 2 hdc in same seam, working in 2nd ch of ch-3 sps on Front and Back and in ends of rows of Shoulders, work 37 [45, 53, 53, 45, 45, 53] 3-hdc groups evenly spaced around neck, join with sl st in 2nd ch of beg ch-2, turn, fasten off. *(38 [46, 54, 54, 46, 46, 54] 3-hdc groups)*

Rnd 2: Working in sps between 3-hdc groups, join turquoise with sc in any sp, ch 3, *sc in next sp, ch 3, rep from * around, join in beg sc, turn, fasten off. *(38 [46, 54, 54, 46, 46, 54] ch sps)*

Rnd 3: Join chocolate in 2nd ch of first ch-3 sp, ch 2, 2 hdc in same ch, 3 hdc in 2nd ch of each ch-3 sp around, join in 2nd ch of beg ch-2, turn, fasten off. *(38 [46, 54, 54, 46, 46, 54] 3-hdc groups)*

Rnd 4: Rep rnd 2.

Rnd 5: Join natural in 2nd ch of first ch-3 sp, ch 2, hdc in same ch, 2 hdc in 2nd ch of each ch-3 sp around, join in 2nd ch of beg ch-2, turn, fasten off. *(38 [46, 54, 54, 46, 46, 54] 2-hdc groups)*

Rnd 6: Working in sps between 3-hdc groups, join turquoise with sc in any sp, ch 2, *sc in next sp, ch 2, rep from * around, join in beg sc, turn, fasten off. *(38 [46, 54, 54, 46, 46, 54] ch sps)*

Rnd 7: Join chocolate in any ch-2 sp, ch 2, 2 hdc in same sp, (sl st, ch 2, 2 hdc) in each ch-3 sp around, join in beg sl st, fasten off.

TUNIC BOTTOM
Rnd 1 (WS): Working on opposite side of Waistband in ends of rows, join turquoise with sc in end of first row, ch 3, *sc in end of next row, ch 3, rep from * around, join in beg sc,

turn, fasten off. *(64 [72, 80, 88, 96, 104, 112] ch sps)*

Rnd 2: Join natural in 2nd ch of first ch-3 sp, ch 2, 2 hdc in same ch, 3 hdc in 2nd ch of each ch-3 sp around, join in 2nd ch of beg ch-2, turn, fasten off. *(64 [72, 80, 88, 96, 104, 112] 3-hdc groups)*

Rnd 3: Working in sps between 3-hdc groups, join turquoise with sc in any sp, ch 3, *sc in next sp, ch 3, rep from * around, join in beg sc, turn, fasten off.

Rnd 4: With chocolate, rep rnd 2.

Rnd 5: With turquoise, rep rnd 3.

Rnd 6: Rep rnd 2. **Do not fasten off**.

Rnd 7: Working in sps between 3-hdc groups, sl st in next sp, ch 1, sc in same sp, *ch 3, sc in 2nd hdc of next 3-hdc group, [ch 3, sc in next sp] 8 [9, 10, 11, 12, 13, 14] times, rep from * around to last 7 [8, 9, 10, 11, 12, 13] sps, ch 3, sc in 2nd hdc of next 3-hdc group, [ch 3, sc in next sp] 7 [8, 9, 10, 11, 12, 13] times, join in beg ch-1, dc in first sc *(counts as a ch-3 sp)*, turn. *(72 [80, 88, 96, 104, 112, 120] ch-3 sps)*

Rnd 8: Ch 1, sc in first ch-3 sp, shell in next ch-3 sp, [sc in next ch-3 sp, ch 3] twice, *sc in next ch-3 sp, shell in next ch-3 sp**, [sc in next ch-3 sp, ch 3] twice, rep from * around, ending last rep at **, sc in next ch-3 sp, ch 3, sc in next ch-3 sp, join in beg ch-1, dc in beg sc, turn. *(18 [20, 22, 24, 26, 28, 30] shells)*

Rnd 9: Ch 1, sc in first ch-3 sp, *ch 3, sc in next ch-3 sp, ch 3, sc in next dc, ch 3, sk next 3 dc, sc in next dc**, ch 3, sc in next ch-3 sp, rep from * around, ending last rep at **, join in beg ch-1, dc in beg sc, turn. *(72 [80, 88, 96, 104, 112, 120] ch-3 sps)*

Rnd 10: Ch 1, sc in first ch-3 sp, *[ch 3, sc in next ch-3 sp] twice, shell in next ch-3 sp**, sc in next ch-3 sp, rep from * around, ending last rep at **, join in beg sc, turn. *(18 [20, 22, 24, 26, 28, 30] shells)*

Rnd 11: Sl st in next dc, ch 1, sc in same dc, *ch 3, sk next 2 dc, sc in next dc, [ch 3, sc in next ch-3 sp] twice**, ch 3, sc in next dc, rep from * around, ending last rep at **, join in beg ch-1, dc in beg sc, turn. *(72 [80, 88, 96, 104, 112, 120] ch-3 sps)*

Rnds 12–31 [12–35, 12–35, 12–35, 12–39, 12–39, 12–39]: [Rep rnds 8–11 consecutively] 5 [6, 6, 6, 7, 7, 7] times.

Medium, Large, 3X-Large & 4X-Large Sizes Only
Fasten off.

Small, X-Large & 2X-Large Sizes Only
Rnds 32 & 33 [36 & 37, 40 & 41]: Rep rnds 8 and 9. Fasten off at end of last rnd.

Bottom Trim
All Sizes
Rnd 1 (RS): Join natural in 2nd ch of first ch-3 sp, ch 2, 2 hdc in same ch, ch 1, (3 hdc, ch 1) in 2nd ch of each ch-3 sp around, join in 2nd ch of beg ch-2, **turn**, fasten off. *(72 [80, 88, 96, 104, 112, 120] 3-hdc groups)*

Rnd 2: Join turquoise with sc in first ch-1 sp, ch 3, *sc in next ch-1 sp, ch 3, rep from * around, join in beg sc, turn, fasten off. *(72 [80, 88, 96, 104, 112, 120] ch sps)*

Rnd 3: Join chocolate in 2nd ch of first ch-3 sp, ch 2, 2 hdc in same ch, 3 hdc in 2nd ch of each ch-3 sp around, join in 2nd ch of beg ch-2, turn, fasten off. *(72 [80, 88, 96, 104, 112, 120] 3-hdc groups)*

Rnd 4: Working in sps between 3-hdc groups, join turquoise with sc in first sp, ch 3, *sc in next sp, ch 3, rep from * around, join in beg sc, turn, fasten off.

Rnd 5: Join natural in 2nd ch of first ch-3 sp, ch 2, 2 hdc in same ch, ch 1, (3 hdc, ch 1) in 2nd ch of each ch-3 sp around, join in 2nd ch of beg ch-2, turn, fasten off. *(72 [80, 88, 96, 104, 112, 120] 3-hdc groups)*

Rnd 6: Rep rnd 2.

Rnd 7: Join chocolate in 2nd ch of any ch-3 sp, ch 2, 3 hdc in same ch, (sl st, ch 2, 3 hdc) in 2nd ch of each ch-3 sp around, join in beg sl st, fasten off.

SLEEVE
Make 2.
Wristband
Row 1: With chocolate, ch 4, 2 dc in 4th ch from hook *(beg 3 sk chs count as first dc)*, turn. *(3 dc)*

Rows 2–27 [2–31, 2–31, 2–35, 2–39, 2–39, 2–43]: Ch 1, sl st in each of first 3 sts, ch 3, 2 dc in same st as last sl st, turn.

Row 28 [32, 32, 36, 40, 40, 44]: Sl st in each of next 3 sts, ch 3, dc in same st as last sl st, sl st in starting ch, dc in same st on last row, fasten off.

Body
Rnd 1 (WS): Working in ends of rows, join turquoise with sc in first row, [ch 3, sc in next row] around, join in beg ch-1, dc in first sc, turn, fasten off. *(28 [32, 32, 36, 40, 40, 44] ch-3 sps)*

Rnd 2: Join natural in 2nd ch of first ch-3 sp, ch 2, 2 hdc in same ch, 3 hdc in 2nd ch of each ch-3 sp around, join in 2nd ch of beg ch-2, turn, fasten off. *(28 [32, 32, 36, 40, 40, 44] 3-hdc groups)*

Rnd 3: Working in sps between 3-hdc groups, join turquoise with sc in first sp, ch 3, *sc in next sp, ch 3, rep from * around, join in beg sc, turn, fasten off. *(28 [32, 32, 36, 40, 40, 44] ch sps)*

Rnd 4: Join chocolate in 2nd ch of first ch-3 sp, ch 2, 2 hdc in same ch, 3 hdc in 2nd ch of each ch-3 sp around, join in 2nd ch of beg ch-2, turn, fasten off. *(28 [32, 32, 36, 40, 40, 44] 3-hdc groups)*

Rnd 5: Rep rnd 3.

Rnd 6: Rep rnd 2.

Rnd 7: Working in sps between 3-hdc groups, join natural with sc in first sp, *ch 3, sc in next sp, rep from * around, join in beg ch-1, dc in beg sc. *(28 [32, 32, 36, 40, 40, 44] ch sps)*

Rnd 8: Ch 1, sc in first ch-3 sp, *[ch 3, sc in next ch-3 sp] twice, shell in next ch-3 sp**, sc in next ch-3 sp, rep from * around, ending last rep at **, join in beg sc, turn. *(14 [16, 16, 18, 20, 20, 22] ch sps, 7 [8, 8, 9, 10, 10, 11] shells)*

Rnd 9: Ch 1, sc in first dc, *ch 3, sk next 3 dc, sc in next dc, [ch 3, sc in next ch-3 sp] twice**, ch 3, sc in next dc, rep from * around, ending last rep at **, join in beg ch-1, dc in beg sc, turn. *(28 [32, 32, 36, 40, 40, 44] ch sps)*

Rnds 10 & 11: Ch 1, sc in first ch-3 sp, *ch 3, sc in next ch-3 sp, rep from * around, join in beg ch-1, dc in beg sc, turn.

Rnd 12: Ch 1, sc in first ch-3 sp, *shell in next ch-3 sp, sc in next ch-3 sp**, [ch 3, sc in next ch-3 sp] twice, rep from * around, ending last rep at **, ch 3, sc in next ch-3 sp, join in beg ch-1, dc in beg sc, turn. *(14 [16, 16, 18, 20, 20, 22] ch sps, 7 [8, 8, 9, 10, 10, 11] shells)*

Rnd 13: Ch 1, sc in first ch-3 sp, *ch 3, sc in next ch-3 sp, ch 3, sc in next dc, ch 3, sk next 3 dc, sc in next dc**, ch 3, sc in next ch-3 sp, rep from * around, ending last rep at **, join in beg ch-1, dc in beg sc, turn. *(28 [32, 32, 36, 40, 40, 44] ch sps)*

Rnds 14 & 15: Rep rnds 10 and 11.

Rnds 16–55: [Rep rnds 8–15 consecutively] 5 times.

Rnds 56–59: Rep rnds 8–11 consecutively.

Sleeve Cap

Row 1: Now working in rows, ch 1, sc in first ch-3 sp, *shell in next ch-3 sp, sc in next ch-3 sp, [ch 3, sc in next ch-3 sp] twice, rep from * 4 [5, 5, 6, 7, 7, 8] times, shell in next ch-3 sp, sc in next ch-3 sp, turn. *(10 [12, 12, 14, 16, 16, 18] ch sps, 6 [7, 7, 8, 9, 9, 10] shells)*

Row 2: Ch 1, sc in next dc, ch 3, sk next 3 dc, sc in next dc,* [ch 3, sc in next ch-3 sp] twice, ch 3, sc in next dc, ch 3, sk next 3 dc, sc in next dc, rep from * across, turn. *(21 [25, 25, 29, 33, 33, 37] ch-3 sps)*

Rows 3 & 4: Ch 3 *(does not count as a st)*, sc in next ch-3 sp, *ch 3, sc in next ch-3 sp, rep from * across to last ch-3 sp, ch 1, dc in 2nd ch of last ch-3 sp *(counts as a ch-3 sp)*, turn. *(19 [23, 23, 27, 31, 31] 5 ch sps at end of last row)*

Row 5: Ch 1, sc in first ch-3 sp, *shell in next ch-3 sp, sc in next ch-3 sp**, [ch 3, sc in next ch-3 sp] twice, rep from * across, ending last rep at **, turn. *(8 [10, 10, 12, 14, 14, 16] ch-3 sps, 5 [6, 6, 7, 8, 8, 9] shells)*

Rows 6–13 [6–17, 6–17, 6–21, 6–21, 6–21, 6–21]: [Rep rows 2–5 consecutively] 2 [3, 3, 4, 4, 4, 4] times. *(4 [4, 4, 4, 6, 6, 6, 8] ch sps, 3 [3, 3, 3, 4, 4, 4, 5] shells)*

Small, 3X-Large & 4X-Large Sizes Only

Rows 14–16 [22–24, 22–24]: Rep rows 2–4. Fasten off at end of last row.

Medium, Large, X-Large & 2X-Large Sizes Only

Rows [18 & 19, 18 & 19, 22 & 23, 22 & 23]: Rep rows 2 and 3 alternately. Fasten off at end of last row.

DRAWSTRING

With 4 strands of chocolate or 2 strands chocolate and 1 strand each of natural and turquoise held tog, ch 200 [220, 240, 260, 290 320, 360]. Fasten off.

FINISHING

Starting at center front, weave Drawstring through Waistband. Matching last row of Sleeves to shoulder seams, sew Sleeves in place. Sew Sleeve seams. •

Garden Kimono

Design by Jill Hanratty

SKILL LEVEL

INTERMEDIATE

FINISHED SIZES

Instructions given fit 32–34-inch bust *(small)*; changes for 36–38-inch bust *(medium)*, 40–42-inch bust *(large)*, 44–46-inch bust *(X-large)*, 48–50-inch bust *(2X-large)* and 52–54-inch bust *(3X-large)* are in [ ].

FINISHED GARMENT MEASUREMENTS

Bust: 44 inches *(small)* [46 inches *(medium)*, 52 inches *(large)*, 54 inches *(X-large)*, 60 inches *(2X-large)*, 62 inches *(3X-large)*]

MATERIALS

- Fingering (super fine) sock yarn: 2200 [2640, 2860, 3300, 3740, 4180] yds desired color

  SUPER FINE

- Size E/4/3.5mm crochet hook or size needed to obtain gauge
- Tapestry needle

GAUGE

1 shell and 1 sc = 2 inches; 6 rows = 2 inches

PATTERN NOTES

Join with a slip stitch unless otherwise stated.

Chain-3 at beginning of first double crochet row or round counts as first double crochet unless otherwise stated.

Chain-4 at beginning of first double crochet row counts as first double crochet and chain-1 space unless otherwise stated.

Chain-6 at beginning of first double crochet row counts as first double crochet and chain-3 space unless otherwise stated.

SPECIAL STITCH

Shell: 11 dc in indicated ch sp.

INSTRUCTIONS

BACK

Row 1 (WS): Beg at top, ch 74 [86, 98, 110, 98, 110], sc in 2nd ch from hook, [ch 3, sk next 5 chs, (dc, ch 5, dc) in next ch, ch 3, sk next 5 chs, sc in next ch] across, turn. *(6 [7, 8, 9, 8, 9] ch-5 sps, 7 [8, 9, 10, 9, 10] sc, 12 [14, 16, 18, 16, 18] ch-3 sps)*

Row 2 (RS): Ch 4 *(see Pattern Notes)*, *sc in next ch-3 sp, **shell** *(see Special Stitch)* in next ch-5 sp, sc in next ch-3 sp**, ch 3, rep from * across, ending last rep at **, ch 1, dc in last st, turn. *(6 [7, 8, 9, 8, 9] shells)*

Row 3: Ch 6, dc in same st, *ch 3, sc in 6th st of next shell, ch 3**, (dc, ch 5, dc) in center ch of next ch-3, rep from * across, ending last rep at **, (dc, ch 3, dc) in last st, turn. *(5 [6, 7, 8, 7, 8] ch-5 sps)*

Row 4: Ch 3, 5 dc in first ch-3 sp, *sc in next ch-3 sp, ch 3, sc in next ch-3 sp*, shell in next ch-5 sp, rep from * across, ending last rep at **, 5 dc in last ch-3 sp, dc in last st, turn. *(5 [6, 7, 8, 7, 8] shells, 2 6-dc groups)*

Row 5: Ch 1, sc in first st, *ch 3, (dc, ch 5, dc) in center ch of next ch-3,

ch 3**, sc in 6th st of next shell, rep from * across, ending last rep at **, sc in last st, turn. *(6 [7, 8, 9, 8, 9] ch-5 sps)*

Rows 6–17 [6–21, 6–25, 6–29, 6–33, 6–33]: [Rep rows 2–5 consecutively] 3 [4, 5, 6, 7, 7] times.

Rows 18 & 19 [22 & 23, 26 & 27, 30 & 31, 34 & 35, 34 & 35]: Rep rows 2 and 3. Fasten off.

FRONT

Row 1: Working on opposite side of starting ch, with RS facing, join with sl st in first ch, ch 3, 5 dc in first ch-5 sp, sc in 3rd ch of same ch-5 sp, *ch 3, sc in 3rd ch of next ch-5 sp**, sk next 2 chs, shell in next ch, sc in 3rd ch of next ch-5 sp, rep from * across, ending last rep at **, 5 dc in same ch sp as last sc, dc in last st, turn. *(5 [6, 7, 8, 7, 8] shells, 2 6-dc groups)*

Row 2: Ch 1, sc in first st, *ch 3, (dc, ch 5, dc) in 2nd ch of next ch-3, ch 3**, sc in 6th dc of next shell, rep from * across, ending last rep at **, sc in last st, turn. *(6 [7, 8, 9, 8, 9] ch-5 sps)*

Right Shoulder

Row 1: Ch 4, [sc in next ch-3 sp, shell in next ch-5 sp, sc in next ch-3 sp, ch 3] 1 [1, 1, 2, 1, 2] times, sc in next ch-3 sp, shell in next ch-5 sp, sc in next ch-3 sp, ch 1, dc in 2nd ch of next ch-3 sp, leaving rem sts unworked, turn. *(2 [2, 2, 3, 2, 3] shells)*

Row 2: Ch 6, dc in same st, *ch 3, sc in 6th dc of next shell, ch 3**, (dc, ch 5, dc) in 2nd ch of next ch-3, rep from * across, ending last rep at **, (dc, ch

3, dc) in last st, turn. *(1 [1, 1, 2, 1, 2] ch-5 sp(s))*

Row 3: Ch 3, 5 dc in next ch-3 sp, *sc in next ch-3 sp, ch 3, sc in next ch-3 sp**, shell in next ch-5 sp, rep from * across, ending last rep at **, 5 dc in last ch sp, dc in last st, turn. *(1 [1, 1, 2, 1, 2] shell(s))*

Row 4: Ch 1, sc in first st, *ch 3, (dc, ch 5, dc) in 2nd ch of next ch-3, ch 3**, sc in 6th st of next shell, rep from * across, ending last rep at **, sc in last st, turn.

Row 5: Ch 4, sc in next ch-3 sp, shell in next ch-5 sp, sc in next ch-3 sp** ch 3, rep from * across, ending last rep at **, ch 1, dc in last st, turn. *(2 [2, 2, 3, 2, 3] shells)*

Rows 6–13 [6–13, 6–13, 6–17, 6–17, 6–21]: [Rep rows 2–5 consecutively] 2 [2, 2, 3, 3, 4] times.

Rows 14 & 15 [14 & 15, 14 & 15, 18 & 19, 18 & 19, 22 & 23]: Rep rows 2 and 3.

Row 16 [16, 16, 20, 20, 24]: Ch 6 *(does not count as first dc and ch-3 sp)*, sc in same st, *ch 3, (dc, ch 5, dc) in 2nd ch of next ch-3, ch 3**, sc in 6th dc of next shell, rep from * across, ending last rep at **, sc in last st, turn. *(2 [2, 2, 3, 2, 3] ch-5 sps)*

Row 17 [17, 17, 21, 21, 25]: Ch 4, *sc in next ch-3 sp, shell in next ch-5 sp, sc in next ch-3 sp, ch 3, rep from * across to last ch-6 sp, sc in last ch-6 sp, turn. *(2 [2, 2, 3, 2, 3] shells)*

Row 18 [18, 18, 22, 22, 26]: Ch 3, *(dc, ch 5, dc) in 2nd ch of next ch 3, ch 3, sc in 6th dc of next shell, ch 3, rep from * across to last st, (dc, ch 3, dc) in last st, turn. *(2 [2, 2, 3, 2, 3] ch-5 sps)*

Row 19 [19, 19, 23, 23, 27]: Ch 3, 5 dc in next ch sp, *sc in next ch-3 sp, ch 3, sc in next ch-3 sp, shell in next ch-5 sp, rep from * across to last st, ch 1, dc in last st, turn. *(2 [2, 2, 3, 2, 3] shells)*

Row 20 [20, 20, 24, 24, 28]: Ch 6, dc in same st, ch 3, *sc in 6th dc of next shell, ch 3, (dc, ch 5, dc) in 2nd ch of next ch-3, ch 3, rep from * across to last 6 dc, sk next 5 dc, sc in last dc, turn. *(2 [2, 2, 3, 2, 3] ch-5 sps)*

Row 21 [21, 21, 25, 25, 29]: Ch 4, sc in next ch-3 sp, *shell in next ch-5 sp, sc in next ch-3 sp, ch 3, sc in next ch-3 sp, rep from * across to last ch-3 sp, 5 dc in last ch-3 sp, dc in last st, turn. *(2 [2, 2, 3, 2, 3] shells)*

Row 22 [22, 22, 26, 26, 30]: Ch 6, sc in same st, ch 3, *(dc, ch 3, dc) in 6th dc of next ch-3, ch 3, sc in 2nd of next shell, ch 3, rep from * across to last st, (dc, ch 3, dc) in last st, turn. *(2 [2, 2, 3, 2, 3] ch-5 sps)*

Row 23 [23, 23, 27, 27, 31]: Ch 3, 5 dc in next ch-3 sp, *sc in next ch-3 sp, ch 3, sc in next ch-3 sp**, shell in next ch-5 sp, rep from * across, ending last rep at **, ch 1, dc in last st, turn. *(2 [2, 2, 3, 2, 3] shells)*

Row 24 [24, 24, 28, 28, 32]: Ch 3, *(dc, ch 5, dc) in 2nd ch of next ch-3, ch 3**, sc in 6th dc of next shell, ch 3, rep from * across, ending last rep at **, sc in last st turn. *(3 [3, 3, 4, 3, 4] ch-5 sps)*

Row 25 [25, 25, 29, 29, 33]: Ch 4, *sc in next ch-3 sp, shell in next ch-5 sp**, sc in next ch-3 sp, ch 3, rep from * across, ending last rep at **, ch 1, dc in last st, turn. *(3 [3, 3, 4, 3, 4] shells)*

Row 26 & 27 [26 & 27, 26 & 27, 30 & 31, 30 & 31, 34 & 35]: Rep rows 2 and 3. *(2 [2, 2, 3, 2, 3] shells at end of last row)*

Row 28 [28, 28, 32, 32, 36]: Ch 6, sc in first st, *ch 3, (dc, ch 3, dc) in center ch of next ch-3 sp, ch 3**, sc in 6th st of next shell, rep from * across, ending last rep at **, sc in last st, turn. *(3 [3, 3, 4, 3, 4] ch-5 sps)*

Row 29 [29, 29, 33, 33, 37]: Ch 4, *sc in next ch-3 sp, shell in next ch-5 sp, sc in next ch-3 sp, ch 3, rep from * across to last ch sp, sc in last ch sp, ch 1, dc in last st, turn. *(3 [3, 3, 4, 3, 4] shells)*

Row 30 [30, 30, 34, 34, 38]: Ch 6, sc in first st, ch 3, *(dc, ch 3, dc) in 2nd ch of next ch-3 sp, ch 3, sc in 6th dc of next shell, ch 3, rep from * across to last st, (dc, ch 3, dc) in last st, turn. *(3 [3, 3, 4, 3, 4] ch-5 sps)*

Row 31 [31, 31, 35, 35, 39]: Ch 3, 5 dc in next ch-3 sp, *sc in next ch-3 sp, ch 3, sc in next ch-3 sp, shell in next ch-5 sp, rep from * across to last ch sp, ch 3, sc in last ch sp, ch 1, dc in last st, turn. *(3 [3, 3, 4, 3, 4] shells)*

Row 32 [32, 32, 36, 36, 40]: Ch 3, *(dc, ch 5, dc) in 2nd ch of next ch-3 sp, ch 3**, sc in 6th dc of next shell, ch 3, rep from * across, ending last rep at **, sc in last st, turn. *(4 [4, 4, 5, 4, 5] ch-5 sps)*

Row 33 [33, 33, 37, 37, 41]: Ch 4, *sc in next ch-3 sp, shell in next ch-5 sp**, sc in next ch-3 sp, ch 3, rep from * across, ending last rep at **, ch 1, sc in last st, turn. *(4 [4, 4, 5, 4, 5] shells)*

Row 34 [34, 34, 38, 38, 42]: Rep row 2.

Small, Medium, X-Large & 3X-Large Sizes Only
Fasten off.

Large & 2X-Large Sizes Only
Rows [35–38, 39–42]: Rep last 4 rows once. Fasten off at end of last row. *([5] shells)*

Left Shoulder
All Sizes

Row 1: Join with sl st in 2nd ch of 7th [7th, 7th, 10th, 7th, 10th] ch sp from end on last row of Front, ch 4, [sc in next ch-3 sp, shell in next ch-5 sp, sc in next ch-3 sp, ch 3] 1 [1, 1, 2, 1, 2] time(s), sc in next ch-3 sp, shell in next ch-5 sp, sc in next ch-3 sp, ch 1, dc in last st, turn. *(2 [2, 2, 3, 2, 3] shells)*

Next rows: Work same as Right Shoulder, reversing shaping.

BODY

Row 1: Working across Left Front, join in first st, ch 3, shell in next ch-3 sp, *sc in next ch-3 sp, ch 3, sc in next ch-3 sp, shell in next ch-5 sp, rep from * across to last 3 ch-3 sps, sc in next ch-3 sp, ch 3, sc in next ch-3 sp, shell in next ch-3 sp, dc in last st, for **armhole**, ch 46 [46, 46, 46, 70, 70], working across last row of Back, dc in first st, shell in next ch-3 sp, *sc in next ch-3 sp, ch 3, sc in next ch-3 sp, shell in next ch-5 sp, rep from * across to last 3 ch-3 sps, sc in next ch-3 sp, ch 3, sc in next ch-3 sp, shell in next ch-3 sp, dc in last st, for **armhole**, ch 46 [46, 46, 46, 70, 70], working across last row of Right Front, dc in first st, shell in next ch-3 sp, *sc in next ch-3 sp, ch 3, sc in next ch-3 sp, shell in next ch-5 sp, rep from * across to last 3 ch-3 sps, sc in next ch-3 sp, ch 3, sc in next ch-3 sp, shell in next ch-3 sp, dc in last st, turn. *(14 [15, 18, 19, 18, 19] shells)*

Row 2: Ch 1, sc in first st, *ch 3, (dc, ch 5, dc) in next ch-5 sp, ch 3, [sc in 2nd ch of next ch-3, ch 3, (dc, ch 5, dc) in next ch-5 sp, ch 3] across to next 6-dc group, dc in last st**, ch 3, sk next 5 chs on armhole, (dc, ch 5, dc) in next ch, ch 3, sk next 5 chs, [sc in next ch, ch 3, sk next 5 chs, (dc, ch 3, dc) in next ch, ch 3, sk next 5 chs] across, sc in next st, rep from * across ending last rep at **, turn. *(22 [23, 26, 27, 30, 31] ch-5 sps)*

Row 3: Ch 4, *sc in next ch-3 sp, shell in next ch-5 sp, sc in next ch-3 sp**, ch 3, rep from * across, ending last rep at **, ch 1, dc in last st, turn. *(22 [23, 26, 27, 30, 31] shells)*

Row 4: Ch 6, dc in same st, *ch 3, sc in 6th dc of next shell, ch 3**, (dc, ch 5, dc) in 2nd ch of next ch-3, rep from * across, ending last rep at **, (dc, ch 3, dc) in last st, turn. *(21 [22, 25, 26, 29, 30] ch-5 sps)*

Row 5: Ch 3, shell in next ch-3 sp, *sc in next ch-3 sp, ch 3, sc in next ch-3 sp**, shell in next ch-5 sp, rep from * across, ending last rep at **, 5 dc in last ch-3 sp, dc in last st, turn. *(21 [22, 25, 26, 29, 30] shells)*

Row 6: Ch 1, sc in first st, *ch 3, (dc, ch 5, dc) in 2nd ch of next ch-3, ch 3**, sc in 6th dc of next shell, rep from * across, ending last rep at **, sc in last st, turn. *(22 [23, 26, 27, 30, 31] ch-5 sps)*

Rows 7–54 [7–58, 7–54, 7–58, 7–54, 7–54]: [Rep rows 3–6 consecutively] 12 [13, 12, 13, 12, 12] times.

Rows 55 & 56 [59 & 60, 55 & 56, 59 & 60, 55 & 56, 55 & 56]: Rep rows 3 and 4.

EDGING

Working around outer edge, with RS facing, ch 3, 6 dc in next ch-3 sp, *dc in next ch-3 sp, ch 3, sc in next ch-3 sp, shell in next ch-5 sp, rep from * across to last 3 ch-3 sps, sc in next ch-3 sp, ch 3, sc in next ch-3 sp, 13 dc in last ch-3 sp, working in ends of rows and in ch sps up next front, across neck edge and down other front, **sc in next row or ch sp, ch 3, sc in next row or ch sp, sk next row *(when working ends of rows only)*, 9 dc in next row or ch sp, rep from ** across to last row, sc in last row, 6 dc in same ch-3 sp as first 6 dc, join in 3rd ch of beg ch-3, fasten off.

SLEEVES

Row 1: Working on 1 armhole ch on Front, join in ch before ends of rows, 6 dc in first row, *sk next row, sc in next row, ch 3, sk next row, sc in next row, sk next row**, shell in next row, rep from * across, ending last rep at **, 6 sc in next row, sl st in st on opposite side of armhole ch, turn. *(8 [9, 10, 11, 12, 12] shells)*

Row 2: Ch 1, sc in first st, *ch 3, (dc, ch 5, dc) in 2nd ch of next ch 3, ch 3**, sc in 6th dc of next shell, rep from * across, ending last rep at **, sc in last st, sk next 2 chs of armhole ch, sl st in next ch, turn. *(9 [10, 11, 12, 13, 13] ch-5 sps)*

Row 3: Ch 4, *sc in next ch-3 sp, shell in next ch-5 sp, sc in next ch-3 sp**, ch 3, rep from * across, ending last rep at **, ch 1, dc in last st, sk next 2 sts on armhole ch, sl st in next ch, turn. *(9 [10, 11, 12, 13, 13] shells)*

Row 4: Ch 6, dc in first dc, *ch 3, sc in 6th dc of next shell, ch 3**, (dc, ch 5, dc) in 2nd ch of next ch-3, rep from * across, ending last rep at **, (dc, ch 3, dc) in last dc, sk next 2 chs on armhole ch, sl st in next ch, turn. *(8 [9, 10, 11, 12, 12] ch-5 sps)*

Row 5: Ch 3, 5 dc in next ch-3 sp, *sc in next ch-3 sp, ch 3, sc in next ch-3 sp**, shell in next ch-5 sp, rep from * across, ending last rep at **, 5 dc in last ch-3 sp, dc in last ch-3 sp, sk next 2 chs on armhole ch, sl st in next ch, turn. *(8 [9, 10, 11, 12, 12] shells)*

Row 6: Ch 1, sc in first dc, *ch 3, (dc, ch 5, dc) in 2nd ch of next ch-3, ch 3**, sc in 6th dc of next shell, rep from * across, ending last rep at **, sc in last dc, sk next 2 chs on armhole ch, sl st in next ch, turn. *(9 [10, 11, 12, 13, 13] ch-5 sps)*

Note: *For last 12 rows on sizes 2X-large and 3X-large, sk 3 chs instead of 2 chs on armhole ch.*

Rows 7–14 [7–14, 7–14, 7–14, 7–18, 7–18]: [Rep rows 3–6 consecutively] 2 [2, 2, 2, 3, 3] times.

Rows 15 & 16 [15 & 16, 15 & 16, 15 & 16, 19 & 20, 19 & 20]: Rep rows 3 and 4.

Rnd 17 [17, 17, 17, 21, 21]: Now working in rnds, ch 3, shell in first ch-3 sp, *sc in next ch-3 sp, ch 3, sc in next ch-3 sp**, shell in next ch-5 sp, rep from * across, ending last rep at **, shell in last ch sp, dc in last st, join in 3rd ch of beg ch-3, **turn.** *(8 [9, 10, 11, 12] shells)*

Rnd 18 [18, 18, 18, 22, 22]: Ch 1, sc in first st, *ch 3, (dc, ch 5, dc) in 2nd ch of next ch-3**, ch 3, sc in 6th dc of next shell, rep from * around, ending last rep at **, ch 1, join with dc in first sc, turn. *(9 [10, 11, 12, 13, 13] ch-5 sps)*

Rnd 19 [19, 19, 19, 23, 23]: Ch 1, sc in sp formed by joining dc, *shell in next ch-5 sp, sc in next ch-3 sp**, ch 3, sc in next ch-3 sp, rep from * around, ending last rep **, ch 1, join with dc in beg sc, turn. *(9 [10, 11, 12, 13, 13] shells)*

Rnd 20 [20, 20, 20, 24, 24]: Ch 6, *sc in 6th dc of next shell, ch 3**, (dc, ch 5, dc) in 2nd ch of next ch-3, ch 3, rep from * around, ending last rep at **, dc in joining dc, ch 2, dc in 3rd ch of beg ch-6, turn. *(8 [9, 10, 11, 12, 12] ch-5 sps)*

Rnd 21 [21, 21, 21, 25, 25]: Ch 3, shell in same sp, *sc in next ch-3 sp, ch 3, sc in next ch-3 sp**, shell in next ch-5 sp, rep from * across, ending last rep at **, shell in next ch-3 sp, ch-3, sl st in 3rd ch of beg ch-3, turn. *(8 [9, 10, 11, 12] shells)*

Rnds 22–49 [22–49, 22–49, 22–53, 26–57, 26–57]: [Rep last 4 rnds consecutively] 7 [7, 7, 8, 8, 8] times.

Rnds 50 & 51 [50 & 51, 50 & 51, 54 & 55, 58 & 59, 58 & 59]: Rep rnds 18 & 19 [18 & 19, 18 & 19, 18 & 19, 22 & 23, 22 & 23]. Fasten off at end of last rnd.

Rep on other armhole.

BELT
First Side
Row 1: Ch 16, 5 dc in 4th ch from hook *(beg 3 sk chs count as first dc)*, sk next 3 chs, sc in next ch, ch 3, sk next 3 chs, sc in next ch, sk next 3 chs, 6 dc in last ch, turn. *(12 dc, 2 sc, 1 ch sp)*

Row 2: Ch 1, sc in first st, ch 3, (dc, ch 5, dc) in next ch-3 sp, ch 3, sc in last st, turn. *(1 ch-5 sp, 2 ch-3 sps)*

Row 3: Ch 4, sc in next ch-3 sp, shell in next ch-5 sp, sc in next ch-3 sp, ch 1, dc in last st, turn. *(1 shell)*

Row 4: Ch 6, dc in same st, ch 3, sc in 6th dc of next shell, ch 3, (dc, ch 3, dc) in last st, turn. *(4 ch-3 sp, 2 ch-3 sps)*

Row 5: Ch 3, 5 dc in first ch-3 sp, sc in next ch-sp, ch 3, sc in next ch-3 sp, 5 dc in next ch-3 sp, dc in last st, turn. *(12 dc, 2 sc, 1 ch sp, 1 ch-3 sp)*

Rows 6–53 [6–57, 6–61, 6–69, 6–73, 6–77]: [Rep rows 2–5 consecutively] 12 [13, 14, 16, 17, 18] times.

Rows 54 & 55 [58 & 59, 62 & 63, 70 & 71, 74 & 75, 78 & 79]: Rep rows 2 and 3. Fasten off at end of last row.

2nd Side
Row 1: Working in starting ch on opposite side of row 1, join in first ch, ch 3, 5 dc in same ch, sk next 3 chs, sc in next ch, ch 3, sk next 3 chs, sc in next ch, sk next 3 chs, 6 dc in last ch, turn.

Next rows: Rep rows 2–55 [2–59, 2–63, 2–71, 2–75, 2–79] of First Side. •

Blooming Cluster Cardigan

Design by Jill Hanratty

SKILL LEVEL

EXPERIENCED

FINISHED SIZES

Instructions given fit 32–34-inch bust *(small)*; changes for 36–38-inch bust *(medium)*, 40–42-inch bust *(large)*, 44–46-inch bust *(X-large)*, 48–50-inch bust *(2X-large)* and 52–54-inch bust *(3X-large)* are in [ ].

FINISHED GARMENT MEASUREMENTS

Bust: 35 inches *(small)* [40 inches *(medium)*, 45 inches *(large)*, 50 inches *(X-large)*, 55 inches *(2X-large)*, 60 inches *(3X-large)*]

MATERIALS

- South West Trading Company Bamboo light (light worsted) weight yarn (3½ oz/250 yds/100g per ball): 4 [4, 5, 5, 5, 5] balls #146 white
- Sizes E/4/3.5mm and G/6/4mm crochet hooks or size needed to obtain gauge
- Tapestry needle

GAUGE

Size G hook: 6 dc = 1 inch; 2 dc rows = 1 inch

PATTERN NOTES

Join with a slip stitch unless otherwise stated.

Chain-3 at beginning of double crochet row counts as first double crochet unless otherwise stated.

Chain-5 at beginning of double

crochet row counts as first double crochet and chain-2 space unless otherwise stated.

Chain-2 at beginning of row does not count as a stitch unless otherwise stated.

2-double crochet cluster (2-dc cl):
Yo, insert hook in indicated st, yo, pull lp through, yo, pull through 2 lps on hook, yo, insert hook in same st, yo, pull lp through, yo, pull through 2 lps on hook, yo, pull through all 3 lps on hook.

3-double crochet cluster (3-dc cl):
Yo, insert hook in indicated st, yo, pull lp through, yo, pull through 2 lps on hook, [yo, insert hook in same st, yo, pull lp through, yo, pull through 2 lps on hook] twice, yo, pull through all 4 lps on hook.

2-treble crochet cluster (2-tr cl):
Yo twice, insert hook in indicated st, yo, pull lp through, [yo, pull through 2 lps on hook] twice, yo twice, insert hook in same st, yo, pull lp through, [yo, pull through 2 lps on hook] twice, yo, pull through all 3 lps on hook.

3-treble crochet cluster (3-tr cl):
Yo twice, insert hook in indicated st, yo, pull lp through, [yo, pull through 2 lps on hook] twice, *yo twice, insert hook in same st, yo, pull lp through, [yo, pull through 2 lps on hook] twice, rep from *, yo, pull through all 4 lps on hook.

Beginning mesh (beg mesh): Ch 5, sk next ch-2 sp, dc in next st.

Mesh: Ch 2, sk next ch sp or 2 sts, dc in next st.

Block: 2 dc in next ch sp, dc in next st, **or**, dc in each of next 3 sts.

INSTRUCTIONS

BODY

Row 1: Beg at bottom, with size G hook, ch 217 [247, 277, 307, 337, 367], dc in 7th ch from hook *(beg 6 sk chs count as dc and ch-2 sp)*, [ch 2, sk next 2 chs, dc in next ch] across, turn. *(71 [81, 91, 101, 111, 121] ch-2 sps)*

Row 2: Ch 5 *(see Pattern Notes)*, sk next ch-sp, *for **lower bloom**, dc in next dc, ch 3, **2-tr cl** *(see Special Stitches)* in top of dc just made, **3-tr cl** *(see Special Stitches)* in next dc, sk next dc, 3-tr cl in next dc, ch 3, 2-tr cl in top of 3-tr cl just made, dc in next dc, ch 2, sk next ch-2 sp, rep from * across to last st, dc in last st, turn. *(14 [16, 18, 20, 22, 24] lower blooms)*

Row 3: Ch 5, sk next ch sp, *dc in next st, for **upper bloom**, ch 2, (3-tr cl, ch 5, 3-tr cl) in next 3-tr cl, ch 2, dc in next st, ch 2, sk next ch sp, rep from * across to last st, dc in last st, turn. *(14 [16, 18, 20, 22, 24] upper blooms)*

Row 4: Ch 5, sk next ch sp, *dc in next st, ch 2, dc in next 3-tr cl, ch 2, dc in 3rd ch of next ch-5, ch 2, dc in next 3-tr cl, ch 2, dc in next dc, ch 2, sk next ch sp, rep from * across to last st, dc in last st, turn. *(71 [81, 91, 101, 111, 121] ch-2 sps, 70 [80, 90, 100, 110, 120] dc)*

Row 5: Ch 5, sk next ch sp, **mesh** *(see Special Stitches)* across, turn. *(71 [81, 91, 101, 111, 121] mesh)*

Row 6: Beg mesh *(see Special Stitches)*, ***block** (see Special Stitches)* 4 times, mesh, rep from * across, turn. *(56 [64, 72, 80, 88, 96] blocks, 15 [17, 19, 21, 23, 25] mesh)*

Row 7: Beg mesh, *block, (ch 2, sk next 2 sts, tr in next st)—mesh made; block, mesh, rep from * across, turn. *(43 [49, 55, 61, 67, 73] mesh, 28 [32, 36, 40, 44, 48] blocks)*

Row 8: Beg mesh, *dc in next st, ch 5, sc in next tr, ch 5, sk next 2 dc, dc in each of next 2 dc, mesh, rep from * across, turn. *(28 [32, 36, 40, 44, 48] ch-5 sps, 15 [17, 19, 21, 23, 35] ch-2 sps)*

Row 9: Beg mesh, *dc in next st, 2 dc in next ch-5 sp, ch 2, tr in next sc, ch 2, 2 dc in next ch-5 sp, dc in each of next 2 sts, mesh, rep from * across, turn. *(43 [49, 55, 61, 67, 73] ch-2 sps, 14 [16, 18, 20, 22, 24] tr)*

Row 10: Beg mesh, *block 4 times, mesh, rep from * across, turn. *(56 [64, 72, 80, 88, 96] blocks, 15 [17, 19, 21, 23, 25] mesh)*

Small, Medium, X-Large & 2X-Large Sizes Only

Row 11: Beg mesh, mesh across, turn. *(71 [81, 91, 101, 111, 121] mesh)*

Large & 3X-Large Sizes Only

Row [11]: Beg mesh, mesh 21 times, [ch 2, sk st or ch, dc in next st or ch] 3 times, mesh across, turn. *([92, 122] mesh)*

Small, Large, X-Large & 3X-Large Sizes Only

Row 12: Ch 2, **3-dc cl** *(see Special Stitches)* in first st, ch 2, **2-dc cl** *(see Special Stitches)* in top of last 3-dc cl made *(half lower bloom made)*, *for **lower blooms**, dc in next st, ch 2, 2-dc cl in top of last dc made, 3-dc cl in each of next 2 dc, ch 3, 2-dc cl in top of last 3-dc cl made, rep from * across to last 2 sts, dc in next st, ch 2, 2-dc cl in top of last dc made, 3-dc cl in last st, turn. *(23 [30, 33, 40] lower blooms, 2 half lower blooms)*

Row 13: Ch 2, for **upper blooms**, 2-dc cl in first 3-dc cl, ch 2, dc in next st, *ch 2, (2-dc cl, ch 2, sl st, ch 2, 2-dc cl) in next 3-dc cl, ch 2, dc in next st, rep from * across to last 3-dc cl, ch 2, 3-dc cl in last 3-dc cl, turn. *(23 [30, 33, 40] upper blooms)*

Medium & 2X-Large Sizes Only

Row [12]: Ch 3, *for **lower blooms**, 2-dc cl in top of last st made, 3-dc cl in each of next 2 sts, ch 2, 2-dc cl in top of last 3-dc cl, dc in next st, rep from * across, turn. *([27, 37] lower blooms)*

Row [13]: Ch 5, (2-dc cl, ch 2, sl st, ch 2, 2-dc cl) in next 3-dc cl, ch 2, dc in next dc, *for **upper blooms**, ch 2, (2-dc cl, ch 2, sl st, ch 2, 2-dc cl) in next 3-dc cl, ch 2, dc in next dc, rep from * across, turn. *([27, 34] upper blooms)*

All Sizes

Row 14: Ch 5, dc in next st, *ch 2, dc in next st, rep from * evenly spaced across 70, 80, 90, 100, 110, 120 times, turn. *(71 [81, 91, 101, 111, 121] ch sps)*

Row 15: Ch 1, sc in first st, *ch 2, sc in next st, rep from * across, turn.

Rows 16–18: Rep rows 6–8.

LEFT FRONT

Row 1: Ch 5, [dc in each of next 2 sts, 2 dc in next ch-5 sp, ch 2, tr in next sc, ch 2, 2 dc in next ch-5 sp, dc in each of next 2 sts, ch 2] 3 [3, 4, 4, 5, 5] times, dc in each of next 2 sts, 2 dc in next ch-5 sp, ch 2, tr in next sc, leaving rem sts unworked, turn. *(11 [11, 14, 14, 17, 17] ch-2 sps)*

Row 2: Ch 3, [2 dc in next ch sp, dc in each of next 4 sts, ch 2, sk next 2 chs, dc in each of next 4 sts, 2 dc in next ch sp, dc in next tr] 3 [4, 5] times, 2 dc in next ch sp, dc in each of next 4 sts, ch 2 in last st, turn. *(47 [47, 60, 60, 73, 73] dc, 4 [4, 5, 5, 6, 6] ch sps)*

Row 3: Ch 2, sk next ch sp, dc in next st, mesh across, turn. *(17 [17, 22, 22, 27, 27] mesh)*

Row 4: Ch 3, sk next ch sp, dc in next dc, mesh twice, *ch 3, 2-tr cl in top of dc just made, 3-tr cl in next dc, sk next dc, 3-tr cl in next dc, ch 3, 2-tr cl in top of 3-tr cl just made, dc in next dc**, ch 2, dc in next st, rep from * across, ending last rep at **, turn. *(3 [3, 4, 4, 5, 5] lower blooms)*

Row 5: Ch 3, *(3-tr cl, ch 5, 3-tr cl) in next 3-tr cl, mesh twice**, ch 2, rep from * across, ending last rep at **, dc in last st, turn. *(3 [3, 4, 4, 5, 5] upper blooms)*

Row 6: Ch 5, sk next dc, dc in next st, *ch 2, dc in next 3-tr cl, ch 2, sc in 3rd ch of next ch-5, ch 2**, dc in next 3-tr cl, mesh twice, rep from * across, ending last rep at **, dc in last st, turn. *(14 [14, 19, 19, 24, 24] ch-2 sps)*

Row 7: Ch 1, dc in next sc, mesh across, turn. *(13 [13, 18, 18, 23, 23] mesh)*

Row 8: Beg mesh, *block 4 times, mesh] across to last 2 ch sps, block, dc in next ch sp, dc in last st, turn. *(9 [9, 13, 13, 17, 17] blocks, 3 [3, 4, 4, 5, 5] mesh)*

Row 9: Sl st in next st, ch 1, dc in next st, *block, mesh, block, ch 2, sk next 2 chs or sts, tr in next st, mesh, rep from * across to last block, block, mesh, turn. *(7 [7, 10, 10, 13, 13] mesh)*

Row 10: Beg mesh, *dc in next st, ch 5, sc in next tr, ch 5, sk next 2 dc, dc in each of next 2 dc, mesh, rep from * across, dc in next st, tr in last st, turn. *(4 [4, 6, 6, 8, 8] ch-5 sps, 3 [3, 4, 4, 5, 5] ch-2 sps)*

Row 11: Ch 1, sk next ch sp, dc in each of next 2 sts, 2 dc in next ch-5 sp, ch 2, tr in next sc, ch 2, 2 dc in next ch-5 sp, dc in each of next 2 sts,

*mesh, dc in next st, 2 dc in next ch-5 sp, ch 2, tr in next sc, ch 2, 2 dc in next ch-5 sp, dc in each of next 2 sts, rep from * across to last mesh, mesh, turn. *(6 [6, 9, 9, 12, 12] ch-2 sps)*

Row 12: Beg mesh, block 4 times, [mesh, block 4 times] across, turn. *(8 [8, 12, 12, 16, 16] blocks)*

Row 13: Ch 3, sk next 2 dc, dc in next dc, mesh across, turn. *(9 [9, 14, 14, 19, 19] mesh)*

Small & Medium Sizes Only

Row 14: Ch 5, 2-dc cl in 3rd ch of ch-5, *3-dc cl in each of next 2 sts, ch 2, 2-dc cl in top of last 3-dc cl made, dc in next st**, ch 2, 2-dc cl in top of last st made, rep from * across, ending last rep at **, turn. *(3 [3] lower blooms)*

Row 15: Ch 5, *(2-dc cl, ch 2, sl st, ch 2, 2-dc cl) in next 3-dc cl, ch 2, dc in next st**, ch 2, rep from * around, ending last rep at **, turn. *(3 [3] upper blooms)*

Large & X-Large Sizes Only

Row [14]: Ch 5, dc in next st, *2-dc cl in top of last dc made, 3-dc cl in each of next 2 sts, ch 2, 2-dc cl in top of last 3-dc cl made, dc in next st, rep from * across to last st, ch 2, dc in last st, turn. *([4] lower blooms)*

Row [15]: Beg mesh, *ch 2, (2-dc cl, ch 2, sl st, ch 2, 2-dc cl) in next 3-dc cl, ch 2, dc in next st, rep from * across, turn. *([4] upper blooms)*

2X-Large & 3X-Large Sizes Only

Row [14]: Ch 5, dc in next st, *2-dc cl in top of last dc made, 3-dc cl in each of next 2 sts, ch 2, 2-dc cl in top of last 3-dc cl made, dc in next st, rep from * across, turn. *([6] lower blooms)*

Row [15]: Ch 5, (2-dc cl, ch 2, sl st,

ch 2, 2-dc cl) in next 3-dc cl, ch 2, dc in next st, *ch 2, (2-dc cl, ch 2, sl st, ch 2, 2-dc cl) in next 3-dc cl, ch 2, dc in next st, rep from * across to last ch sp, turn. ([6] upper blooms)

All Sizes
Row 16: Beg mesh, mesh across turn.

Small, Medium & Large Sizes Only
Fasten off. (9 [9, 14] mesh)

X-Large, 2X-Large & 3X-Large Sizes Only
Row [17]: Ch 2, sk next ch sp, dc in next st, mesh across, turn. ([13, 18, 18] mesh)

X-Large Size Only
Row [18]: Rep row 17. ([12] mesh)

Row [19]: Ch 5, dc in next st, *ch 3, 2-tr cl in top of dc just made, 3-tr cl in next dc, sk next dc, 3-tr cl in next dc, ch 3, 2-tr cl in top of 3-tr cl just made, dc in next dc, mesh, rep from * across to last mesh, mesh, turn. ([2] lower blooms)

Row [20]: Beg mesh, mesh, *ch 2, (3-tr cl, ch 5, 3-tr cl) in next 3-tr cl, ch 2, dc in next st, mesh, rep from * across, turn. ([2] upper blooms)

Row [21]: Ch 1, sc in first st, *ch 3, dc in next dc or 3rd ch of next ch-5, rep from * across, fasten off.

2X-Large & 3X-Large Sizes Only
Row [18]: Beg mesh, mesh across, turn.

Row [19]: Beg mesh, mesh, *ch 3, 2-tr cl in top of dc just made, 3-tr cl in next dc, sk next dc, 3-tr cl in next dc, ch 3, 2-tr cl in top of 3-tr cl just made, dc in next dc, mesh, rep from * across to last mesh, mesh, turn. ([3] lower blooms)

Row [20]: Beg mesh, mesh, *ch 2, (3-tr cl, ch 5, 3-tr cl) in next 3-tr cl, ch 2, dc in next st, mesh, rep from * across to last mesh, mesh, turn. ([3] upper blooms)

Row [21]: Ch 1, sc in first st, *ch 3, dc in next dc or 3rd of next ch-5 sp, rep from * across, fasten off.

RIGHT FRONT
All Sizes
Row 1: With WS facing, join in 4th [4th, 5th, 5th, 6th, 6th] sc from end on Body, ch 5, 2 dc in next ch-5 sp, dc in each of next 2 dc, ch 2, *dc in each of next 2 dc, 2 dc in next ch-5 sp, ch 2, tr in next sc, ch 2, 2 dc in next ch-5 sp, dc in each of next 2 dc, ch 2, rep from * across to last st, dc in last st, turn. (11 [11, 14, 14, 17, 17] ch-2 sps)

Row 2: Beg mesh, *block 4 times, mesh, rep from * across to last 3 dc, block, turn. (14 [14, 18, 18, 22, 22] blocks)

Row 3: Ch 5, dc in next st, mesh across to last block, ch 2, **dc dec** (see Stitch Guide) in next st and last st, turn. (17 [17, 22, 22, 27, 27] mesh)

Row 4: Ch 5, 2-dc cl in 3rd ch of ch-5, 3-tr cl in next dc, sk next dc, 3-tr cl in next dc, ch 3, 2-tr cl in top of 3-tr cl just made, dc in next dc, *mesh, 2-dc cl in 3rd ch of last dc made, 3-tr cl in next dc, sk next dc, 3-tr cl in next dc, ch 3, 2-tr cl in top of 3-tr cl just made, dc in next dc, rep from * across, mesh, ch 2, dc dec in last 2 dc, turn. (3 [3, 4, 4, 5, 5] lower blooms)

Row 5: Ch 2, sk next 2 chs, dc in next st, mesh, *ch 2, (3-tr cl, ch 5, 3-tr cl) in next 3-tr cl**, mesh twice, rep from * across, ending last rep at **, dc in last st, turn. (3 [3, 4, 4, 5, 5] upper blooms)

Row 6: Ch 2, sc in 3rd ch of next ch-5, ch 2, dc in next 3-tr cl, mesh twice, *ch 2, dc in next 3-tr, cl, ch 2, sc in 3rd ch of next ch-5 ch 2, dc in next 3-tr cl, mesh twice, rep from * across, turn. (13 [13, 18, 18, 23, 23] ch-2 sps)

Row 7: Beg mesh, mesh across, turn. (13 [13, 18, 18, 23, 23] mesh)

Row 8: Ch 2, dc in next ch-2 sp, dc in next st, block, mesh, *block 4 times, mesh, rep from * across, turn. (9 [9, 13, 13, 17, 17] blocks, 3 [3, 4, 4, 5, 5] mesh)

Row 9: Ch 5, dc in next st, *block, ch 2, sk next 2 dc, tr in next dc, ch 2, sk next 2 dc, dc in next dc, block, mesh, rep from * across to last block, block, dc in last st, turn. (7 [7, 10, 10, 13, 13] mesh)

Row 10: Ch 4, sk next 2 sts, dc in each of next 2 sts, *ch 2, dc in each of next 2 sts, ch 5, sc in next tr, ch 5, sk next 2 dc, dc in each of next 2 sts, rep from * across to last ch sp, ch 2, dc in last st, turn. (4 [4, 6, 6, 8, 8] ch-5 sps, 3 [3, 4, 4, 5, 5] ch-2 sps)

Row 11: Ch 5, *dc in each of next 2 sts, 2 dc in next ch-5 sp, ch 2, tr in next sc, ch 2, 2 dc in next ch-5 sp, dc in each of next 2 sts, ch 2, rep from * across to last 2 dc, dc dec in last 2 sts, turn. (7 [7, 10, 10, 13, 13] ch-2 sps)

Row 12: Ch 3, sk first 2 chs, dc in next st, *block 4 times, mesh, rep from * across, turn. (8 [8, 12, 12, 16, 16] blocks)

Row 13: Beg mesh, mesh across to last 4 sts, dc dec in next and last st, turn. (9 [9, 14, 14, 19, 19] mesh)

Small & Medium Sizes Only
Row 14: Ch 5, 2-dc cl in 3rd ch of ch-5 sp, sk next ch-2 sp, *3-dc cl in each of next 2 sts, ch 2, 2-dc cl in top of last 3-dc cl made, dc in next st**, ch 2,

2-dc cl in top of last st made, rep from * across, ending last rep at **, turn. *(3 [3] lower blooms)*

Row 15: Ch 5, *(2-dc cl, ch 2, sl st, ch 2, 2-dc cl) in next 3-dc cl, ch 2, dc in next st**, ch 2, rep from * around, ending last rep at **, turn. *(3 [3] upper blooms)*

Large & X-Large Sizes Only
Row [14]: Ch 5, sk next ch sp, dc in next st, *2-dc cl in top of last dc made, 3-dc cl in each of next 2 sts, ch 2, 2-dc cl in top of last 3-dc cl made, dc in next st, rep from * across to last st, ch 2, dc in last st, turn. *([4] lower blooms)*

Row [15]: Beg mesh, *ch 2, (2-dc cl, ch 2, sl st, ch 2, 2-dc cl) in next 3-dc cl, ch 2, dc in next st, rep from * across, turn. *([4] upper blooms)*

2X-Large & 3X-Large Sizes Only
Row [14]: Ch 5, sk next ch sp, dc in next st, *2-dc cl in top of last dc made, 3-dc cl in each of next 2 sts, ch 2, 2-dc cl in top of last 3-dc cl made, dc in next st, rep from * across, turn. *([6] lower blooms)*

Row [15]: Ch 5, (2-dc cl, ch 2, sl st, ch 2, 2-dc cl) in next 3-dc cl, ch 2, dc in next st, *ch 2, (2-dc cl, ch 2, sl st, ch 2, 2-dc cl) in next 3-dc cl, ch 2, dc in next st, rep from * across to last ch sp, turn. *([6] upper blooms)*

All Sizes
Row 16: Beg mesh, mesh across turn.

Small, Medium & Large Sizes Only
Fasten off. *(9 [9, 14] mesh)*

X-Large, 2X-Large & 3X-Large Sizes Only
Row [17]: Ch 2, sk next ch sp, dc in

next st, mesh across, turn. *([13, 18, 18] mesh)*

X-Large Size Only
Row [18]: Rep row 17. *([12] mesh)*

Row [19]: Ch 5, dc in next st, *ch 3, 2-tr cl in top of dc just made, 3-tr cl in next dc, sk next dc, 3-tr cl in next dc, ch 3, 2-tr cl in top of 3-tr cl just made, dc in next dc, mesh, rep from * across to last mesh, mesh, turn. *([2] lower blooms)*

Row [20]: Beg mesh, mesh, *ch 2, (3-tr cl, ch 5, 3-tr cl) in next 3-tr cl, ch 2, dc in next st, mesh, rep from * across, turn. *([2] upper blooms)*

Row [21]: Ch 1, sc in first st, *ch 3, dc in next dc or 3rd ch of next ch-5, rep from * across, fasten off.

BACK
All Sizes
Row 1 (WS): Working from last worked st on Left Front, join in same [next, same, next, same, next] tr, ch 6 *(counts as first tr and ch-2 sp)*, 2 dc in next ch-5 sp, dc in each of next 2 dc, ch 2, *2 dc in each of next 2 sts, 2 dc in next ch-5 sp, ch 2, tr in next sc, ch 2, 2 dc in next ch-5 sp, dc in each of next 2 sts, ch 2, rep from * across to last ch-5 sp, dc in each of next 2 sts, 2 dc in next ch-5 sp, ch 2, tr in next sc, turn. *(21 [21, 24, 24, 27, 27] ch-2 sps)*

Row 2: Ch 3, block twice, mesh, *block 4 times, mesh, rep from * across to last block, block twice, turn. *(7 [7, 9, 9, 11, 11] ch sps)*

Row 3: Ch 2, sk next 2 sts, dc in next st, mesh across to last block, dc in last st, turn. *(34 [34, 39, 39, 44, 44] mesh)*

Row 4: Ch 2, sk next ch sp, dc in next st, mesh twice, *ch 3, 2-tr cl in top

of dc just made, 3-tr cl in next dc, sk next dc, 3-tr cl in next dc, ch 3, 2-tr cl in top of 3-tr cl just made, dc in next dc**, mesh, rep from * across, ending last rep at **, ch 2, dc dec in last 2 sts, turn. *(6 [6, 8, 8, 10, 10] lower blooms)*

Row 5: Beg mesh, *ch 2 (3-tr cl, ch 5, 3-tr cl) in next 3-tr cl, ch 2, dc in next st**, mesh twice, rep from * across, ending last rep at **, mesh, ch 2, dc dec in last 2 sts, turn. *(6 [6, 8, 8, 10, 10] upper blooms)*

Row 6: Beg mesh, *ch 2, dc in next 3-tr cl, ch 2, sc in next 3rd ch of next ch-5, ch 2, dc in next 3-tr cl, mesh twice, rep from * across, turn. *(31 [31, 36, 36, 41, 41] ch-2 sps)*

Row 7: Beg mesh, mesh across, turn.

Rows 8–12: Rep rows 6–10 of Body.

Row 13: Beg mesh, mesh across, turn. *(31 [31, 36, 36, 41, 41] mesh)*

X-Large, 2X-Large & 3X-Large Sizes Only
Rows [14 & 15]: Rep row 13.

Right Shoulder
Small, Medium & Large Sizes Only
Row 1: Ch 5, 2-dc cl in 3rd ch of ch-5, *[3-dc cl in each of next 2 sts, ch 2, 2-dc cl in top of last 3-dc cl made, dc in next st**, ch 2, 2-dc cl in top of last st made] 2 [2, 2] times, 3-dc cl in each of next 2 sts, ch 2, 2-dc cl in top of last 3-dc cl made, dc in next st, sk next 2 chs, tr in next dc, turn. *(3 [3, 3] lower blooms)*

Row 2: Ch 5, *(2-dc cl, ch 2, sl st, ch 2, 2-dc cl) in next 3-dc cl, ch 2, rep from * across to last st, dc in last st, turn. *(3 [3, 3] upper blooms)*

Row 3: Holding Front and Back Shoulders tog, ch 3, sl st in corresponding st on Front, *ch 2, dc in next st on Back, sl st in next st on Front, rep from * across, dc in last st on Back, fasten off.

Left Shoulder
Small, Medium & Large
Sizes Only

Row 1: Join in st before last 10th ch sp on Back, ch 2, sk next 2 ch sps, dc in next st, *ch 3, 2-dc cl in top of last st made, 3-dc cl in each of next 2 sts, ch 2, 2-dc cl in top of last 3-dc cl made, dc in next st, rep from * across, turn. *(3 [3, 3] lower blooms)*

Rows 2 & 3: Rep rows 2 and 3 of Right Shoulder.

Right Shoulder
X-Large, 2X-Large & 3X-Large
Sizes Only

Row [1]: Beg mesh, mesh [10, 15, 15] times, turn. *([11, 16, 16] mesh)*

Row [2]: Beg mesh, *ch 3, 2-tr cl in top of dc just made, 3-tr cl in next dc, sk next dc, 3-tr cl in next dc, ch 3, 2-tr cl in top of 3-tr cl just made, dc in next dc, mesh, rep from * across, turn. *([2, 3, 3] lower blooms)*

Row [3]: Beg mesh, *ch 2, (3-tr cl, ch 5, 3-tr cl) in next 3-tr cl, ch 2, dc in next st, mesh, rep from * across, turn. *([2, 3, 3] upper blooms)*

Row [4]: Beg mesh, *ch 2, dc in next 3-tr cl, ch 2, sc in 3rd ch of next ch-5, ch 2, dc in next 3-tr cl, ch 2, dc next st, rep from * across to last mesh, mesh, turn. *([11, 16, 16] ch sps)*

Row [5]: Holding Front and Back shoulders tog, ch 3, sl st in corresponding st on Front, *ch 2, dc in next st on Back, sl st in next st on Front, rep from* across to last st on Back, dc in last st, fasten off.

Left Shoulder
X-Large, 2X-Large & 3X-Large
Sizes Only

Row [1]: Join in st before last [11, 16, 16] ch sps on Back, beg mesh, mesh across, turn. *([11, 16, 16] ch sps)*

Rows [2–5]: Rep rows [2–5] of Right Shoulder.

SLEEVE
Make 2.

Row 1 (WS): Beg at cuff, ch 52, 52, 67, 82, 82, 97], dc in 7th ch from hook, *ch 2, sk next 2 chs, dc in next ch, rep from * across, turn. *(16 [16, 21, 26, 26, 31] ch sps)*

Row 2: Beg mesh, *ch 3, 2-tr cl in top of dc just made, 3-tr cl in next dc, sk next dc, 3-tr cl in next dc, ch 3, 2-tr cl in top of 3-tr cl just made, dc in next dc, mesh, rep from *across, turn. *(3 [3, 4, 5, 5, 6] lower blooms)*

Row 3: Beg mesh, *ch 2, (3-tr cl, ch 5, 3-tr cl) in next 3-tr cl, ch 2, dc in next st, mesh, rep from * across, turn. *(3 [3, 4, 5, 5, 6] upper blooms)*

Row 4: Ch 5, sk next ch sp, *dc in next st, ch 2, dc in next 3-tr cl, ch 2, dc in 3rd ch of next ch-5, ch 2, dc in next 3-tr cl, ch 2, dc in next dc, ch 2, sk next ch sp, rep from * across to last st, dc in last st, turn. *(16 [16, 21, 26, 26, 31] ch sps)*

Row 5: Beg mesh, mesh across, turn. *(16 [16, 21, 26, 26, 31] mesh)*

Row 6: Ch 5, dc in same st, mesh, *block 4 times, mesh, rep from * across, ch 2, dc in same st as last st, turn. *(12 [12, 16, 20, 20, 24] blocks, 6 [6, 7, 8, 8, 9] mesh)*

Row 7: Beg mesh, mesh, *block, ch 2, sk next 2 sts, tr in next st, mesh, block, mesh, rep from * across to last mesh, mesh, turn. *(12 [12, 15, 18, 18, 21] mesh)*

Row 8: Beg mesh, mesh, *dc in next st, ch 5, sc in next tr, ch 5, sk next 2 dc, dc in each of next 2 dc, mesh, rep from * across to last mesh, mesh, turn. *(6 [6, 8, 10, 10, 12] ch-5 sps, 6 [6, 8, 10, 10, 12] ch-2 sps)*

Row 9: Beg mesh, ch 2, sk next ch sp, *dc in each of next 2 sts, 2 dc in next ch-5 sp, ch 2, tr in next sc, ch 2, 2 tr in next ch-sp, dc in each of next 2 sts, ch 2, rep from * across, dc in next st, mesh, turn. *(12 [12, 15, 18, 18, 21] ch-2 sps)*

Row 10: Beg mesh, mesh, *block 4 times, mesh, rep from * across to last mesh, mesh, turn. *(12 [12, 16, 20, 20, 24] blocks, 6 [6, 7, 8, 8, 9] mesh)*

Row 11: Ch 5, dc in same st, mesh across, ch 2, dc in same st as last st, turn. *(20 [20, 25, 30, 30, 35] mesh)*

Small, Medium &
3X-Large Sizes Only

Row 12: Beg mesh, *ch 2, 2-dc cl, in top of last dc made, 3-dc cl in each of next 2 sts, ch 2, 2-dc cl in top of last 3-dc cl made, dc in next st, rep from * across to last mesh, end mesh, turn. *(6 [6, 11] lower blooms)*

Row 13: Beg mesh, *ch 2, (2-dc cl, ch 2, sl st, ch 2, 2-dc cl) in next 3-dc cl, ch 2, dc in next st, rep from * across to last mesh, mesh, turn. *(6 [6, 11] upper blooms)*

Large Size Only

Row [12]: Ch 5, 2-dc cl, in top of last dc made, *3-dc cl in each of next 2 sts, ch 2, 2-dc cl in top of last 3-dc cl made, dc in next st**, ch 2, 2-dc cl in top of last dc made, rep from * across, ending last rep at **, mesh, turn. *([8] lower blooms)*

Row [13]: Beg mesh, *ch 2, (2-dc cl, ch 2, sl st, ch 2, 2-dc cl) in next

3-dc cl, ch 2, dc in next st, rep from * across, turn. *([8] upper blooms)*

X-Large & 2X-Large Sizes Only

Row [12]: Ch 5, 2-dc cl, in top of last dc made, *3-dc cl in each of next 2 sts, ch 2, 2-dc cl in top of last 3-dc cl made, dc in next st**, ch 2, 2-dc cl in top of last dc made, rep from * across, ending last rep at **, turn. *([10] lower blooms)*

Row [13]: Ch 5, *(2-dc cl, ch 2, sl st, ch 2, 2-dc cl) in next 3-dc cl, ch 2, dc in next st**, ch 2, rep from * across, ending last rep at **, dc in last st, turn. *([10] upper blooms)*

All Sizes

Row 14: Ch 5, dc in same st, mesh across, ch 3, dc in same st as last st, turn. *(22 [22, 27, 32, 32, 37] mesh)*

Row 15: Ch 1, sc in first st, *ch 2, sc in next st, rep from * across, turn. *(22 [22, 27, 32, 32, 37] ch sps)*

Row 16: Ch 3, block 3 times, mesh, *block 4 times, mesh, rep from * across to last 3 ch sps, block 3 times, turn. *(18 [18, 22, 26, 26, 30] blocks, 4 [4, 5, 6, 6, 7] mesh)*

Row 17: Ch 5, sk next 2 sts, tr in next st, mesh, block, *mesh, block, ch 2, sk next 2 sts, tr in next st, mesh**, block, rep from * across, ending last rep at **, turn. *(14 [14, 17, 20, 20, 23] ch sps)*

Row 18: Ch 3, dc in same st, *ch 5, sc in next tr, ch 5**, sk next 4 sts, dc in each of next 2 sts, ch 2, sk next ch sp, dc in each of next 2 sts, rep from * across, ending last rep at **, 2 dc in last st, turn. *(10 [10, 12, 14, 14, 16] ch-5 sps, 4 [4, 5, 6, 6, 7] ch-2 sps)*

Row 19: Ch 3, dc in next st, *2 dc in next ch-5 sp, ch 2, tr in next sc, ch

2, 2 dc in next ch-5 sp, dc in each of next 2 sts**, ch 2, sk next ch sp, dc in each of next 2 sts, rep from * across, ending last rep at **, turn. *(5 [5, 6, 7, 7, 8] tr)*

Row 20: Ch 3, *block 4 times**, mesh, rep from * across, ending last rep at **, turn. *(20 [20, 24, 28, 28, 32] blocks, 4 [4, 5, 6, 6, 7] mesh)*

Row 21: Beg mesh, mesh across, turn. *(24 [24, 29, 34, 34, 39] mesh)*

Row 22: Ch 5, dc in same st, *ch 3, 2-tr cl in top of dc just made, 3-tr cl in next dc, sk next dc, 3-tr cl in next dc, ch 3, 2-tr cl in top of 3-tr cl just made, dc in next dc**, mesh, rep from * across, ending last rep at **, ch 2, dc in same st as last dc, turn. *(5 [5, 6, 7, 7, 8] lower blooms)*

Row 23: Beg mesh, *ch 2, (3-tr cl, ch 5, 3-tr cl) in next 3-tr cl, ch 2, dc in next st, mesh, rep from * across, turn. *(5 [5, 6, 7, 7, 8] upper blooms)*

Row 24: Beg mesh, mesh, ch 2, sc in 3rd ch of next ch-5, *mesh 4 times, ch 2, sc in 3rd ch of next ch-5 sp, rep from * across, mesh 3 times, turn. *(26 [26, 31, 36, 36, 41] ch sps)*

Row 25: Beg mesh, mesh across, turn. *(26 [25, 31, 36, 36, 41] mesh)*

Row 26: Ch 5, dc in same st, mesh, *block 4 times, mesh, rep from * across, ch 3, dc in same st as last dc, turn. *(20 [20, 24, 28, 28, 32] blocks, 8 [8, 9, 10, 10, 11] ch sps)*

Row 27: Beg mesh, mesh, *block, ch 2, sk next 2 sts, tr in next st, mesh, block, mesh, rep from * across to last mesh, mesh, turn. *(18 [18, 21, 24, 24, 27] ch sps)*

Row 28: Beg mesh, *ch 2, dc in each of next 2 sts, ch 5, sc in next tr, ch 5, sk next 2 sts, dc in each of next 2 sts, rep from * across to last 2 mesh, mesh twice, turn. *(10 [10, 12,

14, 14, 16] ch-5 sps, 8 [8, 9, 10, 10, 11] ch-2 sps)*

Row 29: Beg mesh, *ch 2, sk next ch sp, dc in each of next 2 sts, 2 dc in next ch-5 sp, ch 2, tr in next sc, ch 2, 2 dc in next ch-5 sp, dc in each of next 2 sts, rep from * across to last 2 mesh, mesh twice, turn. *(5 [5, 6, 7, 7, 8] tr)*

Row 30: Ch 5, dc in same st, mesh twice, *block 4 times, mesh, rep from * across to last mesh, mesh, ch 2, dc in same st as last dc, turn. *(20 [20, 24, 28, 28, 32] blocks, 10 [10, 11, 12, 12, 13] ch-2 sps)*

Row 31: Beg mesh, mesh across, turn. *(30 [30, 35, 40, 40, 45] mesh)*

Small, Medium & 3X-Large Sizes Only

Row 32: Ch 5, 2-dc cl, in top of last dc made, *3-dc cl in each of next 2 sts, ch 2, 2-dc cl in top of last 3-dc cl made, dc in next st**, ch 2, 2-dc cl in top of last st made, rep from * across, ending last rep at **, turn. *(10 [10, 15] lower blooms)*

Row 33: Ch 5, *(2-dc cl, ch 2, sl st, ch 2, 2-dc cl) in next 3-dc cl, ch 2, dc in next st** ch 2, rep from * across, ending last rep at **, turn. *(10 [10, 15] upper blooms)*

Large Size Only

Row [32]: Beg mesh, *ch 2, 2-dc cl, in top of last dc made, 3-dc cl in each of next 2 sts, ch 2, 2-dc cl in top of last 3-dc cl made, dc in next st, rep from * across to last mesh, end mesh, turn. *([11] lower blooms)*

Row [33]: Beg mesh, *ch 2, (2-dc cl, ch 2, sl st, ch 2, 2-dc cl) in next 3-dc cl, ch 2, dc in next st, rep from * across to last mesh, mesh, turn. *([11] upper blooms)*

X-Large & 2X-Large Sizes Only

Row [32]: Ch 5, 2-dc cl, in top of last dc made, *3-dc cl in each of next 2 sts, ch 2, 2-dc cl in top of last 3-dc cl made, dc in next st**, ch 2, 2-dc cl in top of last dc made, rep from * across, ending last rep at **, mesh, turn. *([13] lower blooms)*

Row [33]: Beg mesh, *ch 2, (2-dc cl, ch 2, sl st, ch 2, 2-dc cl) in next 3-dc cl, ch 2, dc in next st, rep from * across, turn. *([13] upper blooms)*

All Sizes

Row 34: Beg mesh, mesh across, turn. *(30 [30, 35, 40, 40, 45] mesh)*

Row 35: Ch 1, sc in first st, *ch 2, sc in next st, rep from * across, turn. *(30 [30, 35, 40, 40, 45] ch sps)*

Row 36: Ch 3, block twice, mesh, *block 4 times, mesh, rep from * across to last 2 ch sps, block twice, turn. *(24 [24, 28, 32, 32, 36] blocks, 6 [6, 7, 8, 8, 9] mesh)*

Row 37: Ch 6 *(counts as first tr and ch-2 sp)*, dc in next st, block, *mesh, block**, ch 2, sk next 2 sts, tr in next st, mesh, block, rep from * across, ending last rep at **, ch 2, tr in last st, turn. *(7 [7, 8, 9, 9, 10] tr)*

Row 38: Ch 1, sc in first st, ch 5, sk next 2 dc, dc in each of next 2 dc, *ch 2, sk next ch sp, dc in each of next 2 sts**, ch 5, sc in next tr, ch 5, sk next 2 sts, dc in each of next 2 sts, rep from * across, ending last rep at **, ch 5, sc in last tr. Fasten off. *(12 [12, 14, 16, 16, 18] ch-5 sps)*

SLEEVE CAP

Row 1 (WS): Join in 2nd ch-5 sp, ch 5, *tr in next sc, ch 2**, 2 dc in next ch-5 sp, dc in each of next 2 sts, ch 2, sk next ch sp, dc in each of next 2 sts, 2 dc in next ch-5 sp, ch 2, rep from * across, ending last rep at ** before next to last ch-5 sp, dc in next ch-5 sp, turn. *(14 [14, 17, 20, 20, 23] ch-2 sps)*

Row 2: Ch 2, dc in next tr, block twice, *mesh, block 4 times, rep from * across to last 3 ch sps, mesh, block twice, leaving rem sts unworked, turn. *(4 [4, 5, 6, 6, 7] ch-2 sps)*

Row 3: Beg mesh, mesh 19 [19, 24, 27, 27, 31] times, turn. *(20 [20, 25, 28, 28, 32] mesh)*

Row 4: Ch 2, dc in next st, mesh twice, *ch 3, 2-tr cl in top of dc just made, 3-tr cl in next dc, sk next dc, 3-tr cl in next dc, ch 3, 2-tr cl in top of 3-tr cl just made, dc in next dc, mesh, ch 2, dc dec in last 2 sts, turn. *(3 [3, 4, 5, 5, 6] lower blooms)*

Row 5: Ch 2, dc in next st, mesh, *ch 2, (3-tr cl, ch 5, 3-tr cl) in next 3-tr cl, ch 2, dc in next st**, mesh, rep from * across, ending last rep at **, ch 2, dc dec in last 2 sts, turn. *(3 [3, 4, 5, 5, 6] upper blooms)*

Row 6: Ch 2, dc in next st, *ch 2, dc in next 3-tr cl, ch 2, sc in 3rd ch of next ch-5, ch 2, dc in next 3-tr cl**, ch 2, dc in next dc, mesh, rep from * across, end last rep at **, ch 2, dc dec in last 2 sts, turn. *(14 [14, 19, 24, 24, 29] ch sps)*

Row 7: Ch 2, dc in next st, mesh across to last 2 sts, ch 2, dc dec in last 2 sts, turn. *(12 [12, 17, 22, 22, 27] mesh)*

Small Size Only

Row 8: Rep row 7. Fasten off.

Medium Size Only

Row [8]: Ch 5, *2-dc cl in top of last dc made, 3-dc cl in each of next 2 sts, ch 2, 2-dc cl in top of last 3-dc cl made, dc in next st**, ch 2, rep from * across, ending last rep at **, turn. *([4] lower blooms)*

Row [9]: Ch 5, *(2-dc cl, ch 2, sl st, ch 2, 2-dc cl) in next 3-dc cl, ch 2, dc in next st** ch 2, rep from * across, ending last rep at **, turn. *([4] upper blooms)*

Row [10]: Ch 2, sc in next st, [ch 2, sc in next st] 10 times, leaving rem sts unworked, fasten off.

Large Size Only

Row [8]: Ch 2, dc in next st, *ch 2, 2-dc cl in top of last dc made, 3-dc cl in each of next 2 sts, ch 2, 2-dc cl in top of last 3-dc cl made**, dc in next st, rep from * across, ending last rep at **, dc dec in last 2 sts, turn. *([5] lower blooms)*

Row [9]: Ch 5, *(2-dc cl, ch 2, sl st, ch 2, 2-dc cl) in next 3-dc cl, ch 2, dc in next st** ch 2, rep from * across, ending last rep at **, turn. *([5] upper blooms)*

Row [10]: Ch 2, sc in next st, [ch 2, sc in next st] 10 times, leaving rem sts unworked, fasten off.

X-Large, 2X-Large & 3X-Large Sizes Only

Row [8]: Ch 2, dc in next st, block twice, mesh, *block 4 times, mesh, rep from * across to last 3 ch sps, block twice, leaving rem sts unworked, turn. *([16, 16, 20] blocks, [4, 4, 5] mesh)*

Row [9]: Ch 2, sk next 2 sts, dc in next st, block, mesh, *block, ch 2, sk next 2 sts, tr in next st, mesh, block, mesh, rep from * across to last 2 blocks, dc in each of next 2 sts, dc dec in next and last st, turn. *([10, 10, 13] ch sps)*

Row [10]: Ch 1, sk first 2 sts, dc in each of next 2 sts, *ch 2, sk next ch sp, dc in each of next 2 sts**, ch 5, sc in next tr, ch 5, sk next 2 sts, dc in each of next 2 sts, rep from * across, ending last rep at **, leaving rem sts unworked, turn. *([6, 6, 8] ch-5 sps, [4, 4, 5] ch-2 sps)*

Row [11]: Ch 2, dc in next st, *ch 2, sk next ch sp**, dc in each of next 2 sts, 2 dc in next ch-5 sp, ch 2, tr in next sc, ch 2, 2 dc in next ch-5 sp, dc in each of next 2 sts, rep from * across, ending last rep at**, dc dec in last 2 sts, turn. *([10, 10, 13] ch sps)*

Row [12]: Ch 2, sk next ch sp, dc in next st, [block 4 times, mesh] [2, 2, 3] times, block 3 times, dc in each of next 2 sts, dc dec in next and last st, turn. *([12, 12, 15] blocks, [2, 2, 3] mesh)*

Row [13]: Ch 2, sk next 2 sts, dc in next st, mesh across, fasten off. *([13, 13, 18] mesh)*

ASSEMBLY

Easing to fit, sew shoulder seams. Matching last row of Sleeves to shoulder seams, sew Sleeves in place. Sew Sleeve seams.

BOTTOM & FRONT TRIM

With RS facing, working in starting ch on opposite side of row 1 on Fronts and Back, join with sc in ch sp at bottom corner of Left Front, 2 sc in same sp, *3 hdc in next ch sp, (3 dc, tr) in next ch sp, tr in next ch, (tr, 3 dc) in next ch sp, 3 hdc in next ch sp, 3 sc in next ch sp, rep from * across to bottom corner of Right Front, working in ends of rows and ch sps across Fronts and neck edge, 3 sc in each ch sp around, join in beg sc, fasten off.

SLEEVE TRIM

Working in starting ch on opposite side of row 1 on Sleeve, join in seam, *3 sc in next ch sp, 3 hdc in next ch sp, (3 dc, 1 tr) in next ch sp, tr in next ch, (tr, 3 dc) in next ch sp, 3 hdc in next ch sp, rep from * around, join in beg sc, fasten off. Rep on other Sleeve.

BUTTON

Ch 4, 16 dc in 3rd ch from hook, join with sl st in 3rd ch of beg ch-3 Fasten off, leaving long strand for weaving. Weave strand through sts, pull to gather tightly, secure end.

FINISHING

Sew button to Left Front using sps between sts on Right Front as buttonhole. •

Southwest Shimmer Jacket

Design by Jill Hanratty

SKILL LEVEL

INTERMEDIATE

FINISHED SIZES

Instructions given fit 32–34-inch bust *(small)*; changes for 36–38-inch bust *(medium)*, 40–42-inch bust *(large)*, 44–46-inch bust *(X-large)*, 48–50-inch bust *(2X-large)* and 52–54-inch bust *(3X-large)* are in [ ].

FINISHED GARMENT MEASUREMENTS

Bust: 35 inches *(small)* [40 inches *(medium)*, 45 inches *(large)*, 50 inches *(X-large)*, 55 inches *(2X-large)*, 60 inches *(3X-large)*]

MATERIALS

- Berroco Cotton Twist Variegated medium (worsted) weight yarn (1¾ oz/85 yds/50g per hank): 8 [9, 10, 11, 12, 14] hanks #8482 be bop
- Size H/8/5mm crochet hook or size needed to obtain gauge
- Tapestry needle

GAUGE

4 shells and 4 sc = 5 inches; 8 shell rows = 7 inches

PATTERN NOTES

Chain-5 at beginning of double crochet row counts as first double crochet and chain-2 space unless otherwise stated.

Chain-4 at beginning of double crochet row counts as first double

crochet and chain-1 space unless otherwise stated.

Chain-3 at beginning of double crochet row counts as first double crochet unless otherwise stated.

SPECIAL STITCHES

Beginning shell (beg shell): Ch 4, (dc, ch 1, dc) in stitch indicated.

Shell: (Dc, {ch 1, dc} twice) in stitch indicated.

INSTRUCTIONS

LEFT FRONT

Row 1: Ch 38 [44, 50, 56, 62, 68], sc in 2nd ch from hook, [sk next 2 chs, **shell** (see Special Stitches) in next ch, sk next 2 chs, sc in next ch] across, turn. (6 [7, 8, 9, 10, 11] shells)

Row 2: Ch 5 (see Pattern Notes), sc in 2nd dc of next shell, *ch 5, sc in 2nd dc of next shell, rep from * across to last sc, ch 2, dc in last sc, turn. (5 [6, 7, 8, 9, 10] ch-5 sps, 6 [7, 8, 9, 10, 11] sc)

Row 3: Ch 1, sc in first st, shell in next sc, *sc in next ch-5 sp, shell in next sc, rep from * across to last st, sc in last st, turn. (6 [7, 8, 9, 10, 11] shells, 8 [9, 10, 11, 12, 13] sc)

Row 4: Ch 5, sc in 2nd dc of next shell, *ch 5, sc in 2nd dc of next shell, rep from * across to last sc, ch 2, (dc, ch 1, dc) in last sc, turn. (5 [6, 7, 8, 9, 10] ch-5 sps, 6 [7, 8, 9, 10, 11] sc)

Row 5: Ch 4 (see Pattern Notes), dc in same st, sc in next dc, shell in next sc, *sc in next ch-5 sp, shell in next sc, rep from * across to last st, sc in last st, turn. (6 [7, 8, 9, 10, 11] shells, 8 [9, 10, 11, 12, 13] sc)

Row 6: Ch 5, sc in 2nd st of next shell, *ch 5, sc in 2nd st of next shell,

rep from * across to last st, ch 5, sc in last st, turn. (6 [7, 8, 9, 10, 11] ch-5 sps, 7 [8, 9, 10, 11, 12] sc)

Row 7: Beg shell (see Special Stitches) in first st, *sc in next ch-5 sp, shell in next sc, rep from * across to last st, sc in last st, turn. (7 [8, 9, 10, 11, 12] shells, 8 [9, 10, 11, 12, 13] sc)

Row 8: Ch 5, *sc in 2nd dc of next shell, ch 5, rep from * across to last shell, sc in 2nd dc of last shell, ch 2, dc in last st, turn. (6 [7, 8, 9, 10, 11] ch-5 sps, 7 [8, 9, 10, 11, 12] sc, 1 dc)

Small, Medium & Large Sizes Only

Rows 9 & 10 [9 & 10, 9 & 10]: Rep rows 3 and 2.

All Sizes

Rows 11 & 12 [11 & 12, 11 & 12, 9 & 10, 9 & 10, 9 & 10]: Rep rows 3 and 2.

Row 13 [13, 13, 11, 11, 11]: Ch 1, sc in first st, *shell in next sc, sc in next sp, rep from * across to last sc, dc in last sc, ch 1, dc in last st, turn. (6 [7, 8, 9, 10, 11] shells, 7 [8, 9, 10, 11, 12] sc, 1 dc)

Row 14 [14, 14, 12, 12, 12]: Ch 1, sc in first st, *ch 5, sc in 2nd dc of next shell, rep from * across, ch 2, dc in last st, turn, fasten off. (6 [7, 8, 9, 10, 11] ch-5 sps, 7 [8, 9, 10, 11, 12] sc, 1 dc)

Row 15 [15, 15, 13, 13, 13]: Join with sc in center ch of first [2nd, 3rd, 3rd, 4th, 5th] ch-5 sp, *shell in next sc, sc in next ch-5 sp, rep from * across to last st, dc in last st, turn. (5 [5, 5, 6, 6, 6] shells, 7 [7, 7, 8, 8, 8] sc, 1 dc)

Row 16 [16, 16, 14, 14, 14]: Ch 1, sc in first st, *ch 5, sc in 2nd st of next shell, rep from * across to last st, ch 2, dc in last st, turn. (5 [5, 5, 6, 6, 6] ch-5 sps, 6 [6, 6, 7, 7, 7] sc, 1 dc)

Row 17 [17, 17, 15, 15, 15]: Ch 1, sc in first st, *shell in next sc, sc in next ch-5 sp, rep from * across to last st, ch 2, dc in last st, turn. (5 [5, 5, 6, 6, 6] shells, 6 [6, 6, 7, 7, 7] sc, 1 dc)

Rows 18–23 [18–23, 18–23, 16–21, 16–21, 16–21]: [Rep rows 2 and 3 alternately] 3 times.

Row 24 [24, 24, 22, 22, 22]: Rep row 2.

Row 25 [25, 25, 23, 23, 23]: Rep row 13 [13, 13, 11, 11, 11]. (4 [4, 4, 5, 5, 5] shells, 5 [5, 5, 6, 6, 6] sc, 1 dc)

Row 26 [26, 26, 24, 24, 24]: Rep row 16 [16, 16, 14, 14, 14]. (4 [4, 4, 5, 5, 5] ch-5 sps, 5 [5, 5, 6, 6, 6] sc, 1 dc)

Row 27 [27, 27, 25, 25, 25]: Ch 1, sc in first st, *shell in next sc, sc in next ch-5 sp, rep from * across to last st, dc in last st, turn. (4 [4, 4, 5, 5, 5] shells, 5 [5, 5, 6, 6, 6] sc, 1 dc)

Rows 28 & 29 [28–31, 28–33, 26–35, 26–37, 26–39]: [Rep rows 2 and 3 alternately] 1 [2, 3, 5, 6, 7] times. Fasten off at end of last row.

RIGHT FRONT

Row 1: Ch 38 [44, 50, 56, 62, 68], sc in 2nd ch from hook, *sk next 2 chs, shell in next ch, sk next 2 chs, sc in next ch, rep from * across, turn. (6 [7, 8, 9, 10, 11] shells)

Row 2: Ch 5, sc in 2nd dc of next shell, *ch 5, sc in 2nd dc of next shell, rep from * across to last sc, ch 2, dc in last sc, turn. (5 [6, 7, 8, 9, 10] ch-5 sps, 6 [7, 8, 9, 10, 11] sc)

Row 3: Ch 1, sc in first st, shell in next sc, *sc in next ch-5 sp, shell in next sc, rep from * across to last st, sc in last st, turn. (6 [7, 8, 9, 10, 11] shells, 8 [9, 10, 11, 12, 13] sc)

Row 4: Ch 4, dc in same st, ch 2, sc in 2nd st of next shell, *ch 5, sc in 2nd dc of next shell, rep from * across to

last st, ch 2, dc in last st, turn.
(5 [6, 7, 8, 9, 10] ch-5 sps, 6 [7, 8, 9, 10, 11] sc)

Row 5: Ch 1, sc in first st, shell in next sc, *sc in next ch-5 sp, shell in next sc, rep from * across to last 2 sts, sc in next st, (dc, ch 1, dc) in last st, turn. *(6 [7, 8, 9, 10, 11] shells, 8 [9, 10, 11, 12, 13] sc)*

Row 6: Ch 1, sc in first st, *ch 5, sc in 2nd dc of next shell, rep from * across to last st, ch 2, dc in last st, turn. *(6 [7, 8, 9, 10, 11] ch-5 sps, 7 [8, 9, 10, 11, 12] sc)*

Row 7: Ch 1, sc in first st, shell in next sc, *sc in next ch-5 sp, shell in next sc, rep from * across, turn. *(7 [8, 9, 10, 11, 12] shells, 8 [9, 10, 11, 12, 13] sc)*

Row 8: Ch 5, sc in 2nd dc of first shell, *ch 5, sc in 2nd dc of next shell, rep from * across to last st, ch 2, dc in last st, turn. *(6 [7, 8, 9, 10, 11] ch-5 sps, 7 [8, 9, 10, 11, 12] sc)*

Row 9: Ch 1, sc in first st, shell in next sc, *sc in next ch-5 sp, shell in next sc, rep from * across to last st, sc in last st, turn. *(7 [8, 9, 10, 11, 12] shells, 8 [9, 10, 11, 12, 13] sc)*

Small, Medium & Large Sizes Only

Rows 10 & 11 [10 & 11, 10 & 11]: Rep rows 2 and 9.

All Sizes

Row 12 [12, 12, 10, 10, 10]: Ch 5, sc in 2nd dc of next shell, *ch 5, sc in 2nd dc on next shell, rep from * across to last st, dc in last st, turn. *(6 [7, 8, 9, 10, 11] ch-5 sps, 7 [8, 9, 10, 11, 12] sc, 1 dc)*

Row 13 [13, 13, 11, 11, 11]: Ch 4, dc in same st, *sc in next ch-5 sp, shell in next sc, rep from * across to last st,

sc in last st, turn. *(6 [7, 8, 9, 10, 11] shells, 7 [8, 9, 10, 11, 12] sc, 2 dc)*

Row 14 [14, 14, 12, 12, 12]: Ch 5, *sc in 2nd dc of next shell, ch 5, rep from * across to last st, sc in last st, turn. *(6 [7, 8, 9, 10, 11] ch-5 sps, 7 [8, 9, 10, 11, 12] sc)*

Armhole Shaping
Row 15 [15, 15, 13, 13, 13]: Ch 3 *(see Pattern Notes)*, [sc in next ch-5 sp, shell in next sc] 5 [5, 5, 6, 6, 6] times, sc in 3rd ch of next ch-5 sp, leaving rem sts unworked, turn. *(5 [5, 5, 6, 6, 6] shells, 6 [6, 6, 7, 7, 7] sc, 1 dc)*

Row 16 [16, 16, 14, 14, 14]: Ch 5, sc in 2nd dc of next shell, *ch 5, sc in 2nd dc of next shell, rep from * across to last st, ch 2, dc in last st, turn. *(4 [4, 4, 5, 5, 5] ch-5 sps, 5 [5, 5, 6, 6, 6] sc, 1 dc)*

Row 17 [17, 17, 15, 15, 15]: Rep row 9. *(5 [5, 5, 6, 6, 6] shells)*

Rows 18–23 [18–23, 18–23, 16–21, 16–21, 16–21]: [Rep rows 2 and 9 alternately] 3 times.

Row 24 [24, 24, 22, 22, 22]: Ch 5, sc in 2nd dc of next shell, *ch 5, sc in 2nd dc of next shell, rep from * across to last st, dc in last st, turn. *(4 [4, 4, 5, 5, 5] ch-5 sps, 5 [5, 5, 6, 6, 6] sc, 1 dc)*

Row 25 [25, 25, 23, 23, 23]: Ch 4, dc in same st, *sc in next ch-5 sp, shell in next sc, rep from * across to last st, sc in last st, turn. *(4 [4, 4, 5, 5, 5] shells, 5 [5, 5, 6, 6, 6] sc, 1 dc)*

Row 26 [26, 26, 24, 24, 24]: Ch 5, *sc in 2nd dc of next shell, ch 5, rep from * across to last st, sc in last st, turn. *(4 [4, 4, 5, 5, 5] ch-5 sps, 5 [5, 5, 6, 6, 6] sc, 1 dc)*

Row 27 [27, 27, 25, 25, 25]: Ch 3, *sc in next ch 5 sp, shell in next sc, rep from * across, sc in last st, turn. *(4 [4, 4, 5, 5, 5] shells, 5 [5, 5, 6, 6, 6] sc)*

Row 28 [28, 28, 26, 26, 26]: Ch 5, sc in 2nd dc of next shell, *ch 5, sc in 2nd dc of next shell, rep from * across to last st, ch 2, dc in last st, turn. *(3 [3, 3, 4, 4, 4] ch-5 sps, 4 [4, 4, 5, 5, 5] sc, 1 dc)*

Small Size Only
Row 29: Rep row 9. Fasten off.

Medium, Large, X-Large, 2X-Large & 3X-Large Sizes Only
Row [29, 29, 27, 27, 27]: Rep row 9.
Rows [30 & 31, 30–33, 28–35, 28–37, 28–39]: [Rep rows 2 and 9 alternately] [1, 2, 4, 5, 6] times. Fasten off at end of last row.

BACK
All Sizes
Row 1: Ch 74 [86, 98, 110, 122, 134], sc in 2nd ch from hook, *sk next 2 chs, shell in next ch, sk next 2 chs, sc in next ch, rep from * across, turn. *(12 [14, 16, 18, 20, 22] shells, 14 [16, 18, 20, 22, 24] sc)*

Row 2: Ch 5, sc in 2nd dc of next shell, *ch 5, sc in 2nd dc of next shell, rep from * across to last sc, ch 2, dc in last sc, turn. *(11 [13, 15, 17, 19, 21] ch-5 sps, 12 [14, 16, 18, 20, 22] sc, 1 dc)*

Row 3: Ch 1, sc in first st, shell in next sc, *sc in next ch-5 sp, shell in next sc, rep from * across to last sc, sc in last st, turn. *(12 [14, 16, 18, 20, 22] shells, 13 [15, 17, 19, 21, 23] sc)*

Row 4: Ch 4, dc in same st, ch 2, sc in 2nd dc of next shell, *ch 5, sc in 2nd dc of next shell, rep from * across to last st, ch 2, (dc, ch 1, dc) in last st, turn. *(11 [13, 15, 17, 19, 21] ch-5 sps, 12 [14, 16, 18, 20, 22] sc, 4 dc)*

Row 5: Ch 4, dc in same st, sc in next dc, shell in next sc, *sc in next ch-5

sp, shell in next sc, rep from * across to last 2 sts, sc in next dc, (dc, ch 1, dc) in last st, turn. *(12 [14, 16, 18, 20, 22] shells, 13 [15, 17, 19, 21, 23] sc, 4 dc)*

Row 6: Ch 1, sc in first st, ch 5, *sc in 2nd dc of next shell, ch 5, rep from * across to last st, sc in last st, turn. *(13 [15, 17, 19, 21, 23] ch-5 sps, 14 [16, 18, 20, 22, 24] sc)*

Row 7: Ch 4, (dc, ch 1, dc) in first st, *sc in next ch-5 sp, shell in next sc, rep from * across, turn. *(14 [16, 18, 20, 22, 24] shells, 13 [15, 17, 19, 21, 23] sc)*

Row 8: Ch 5, sc in 2nd dc of first shell, *ch 5, sc in 2nd dc of next shell, rep from * across, ch 2, dc in last st of same shell, turn. *(13 [15, 17, 19, 21, 23] ch-5 sps, 14 [16, 18, 20, 22, 24] sc, 1 dc)*

Row 9: Ch 1, sc in first st, shell in next sc, *sc in next ch-5 sp, shell in next sc, rep from * across to last st, sc in last st, turn. *(14 [16, 18, 20, 22, 24] shells, 15 [17, 19, 21, 23, 25] sc)*

Rows 10–13 [10–13, 10–13, 10 & 11, 10 & 11, 10 & 11]: [Rep rows 2 and 9 alternately] 2 [2, 2, 1, 1, 1] time(s).

Row 14 [14, 14, 12, 12, 12]: Rep row 2. Fasten off.

Row 15 [15, 15, 13, 13, 13]: Join yarn with sc in center ch of first [2nd, 3rd, 3rd, 4th, 5th] ch-5, *shell in next sc, sc in next ch-5 sp, rep from * across, leaving last 0 [1, 2, 2, 3, 4] ch-5 sp(s) unworked, turn. *(12 [12, 12, 14, 14, 14] shells, 13 [13, 13, 15, 15, 15] sc)*

Next rows: [Rep rows 2 and 9 alternately] 6 [7, 8, 10, 11, 12] times.

Left Shoulder
Row 1: Ch 5, sc in 2nd dc of first shell, [ch 5, sc in 2nd dc of next shell] 3 [3, 3, 4, 4, 4] times, ch 2, dc in next sc,

leaving rem sts unworked, turn. *(3 [3, 3, 4, 4, 4] ch-5 sps, 4 [4, 4, 5, 5, 5] sc)*

Row 2: Ch 1, sc in first st, shell in next st, *sc in next ch-5 sp, shell in next sc, rep from * across to last st, sc in last st, turn. *(4 [4, 4, 5, 5, 5] shells, 5 [5, 5, 6, 6, 6] sc)*

Row 3: For **joining**, sl st in first sc on RS of Left Front, [ch 2, sl st in 2nd dc of next shell on WS of Back, sl st in 2nd dc of corresponding shell on RS of Left Front, ch 2, sl st in next sc on WS of Left Back] 4 [4, 4, 5, 5, 5] times, ch 2, sl st in last sc on RS of Left Front, fasten off.

Right Shoulder

Row 1: Sk next 4 [4, 4, 5, 5, 5] shells on last row of Back, join with sl st in next sc, ch 5, sc in 2nd dc of next shell, *ch 5, sc in 2nd dc of next shell, rep from * across to last st, ch 2, dc in last st, turn. *(3 [3, 3, 4, 4, 4] ch-5 sps, 4 [4, 4, 5, 5, 5] sc)*

Row 2: Ch 1, sc in first st, shell in next st, *sc in next ch-5 sp, shell in next sc, rep from * across to last st, sc in last st, turn. *(4 [4, 4, 5, 5, 5] shells, 5 [5, 5, 6, 6, 6] sc)*

Row 3: For **joining**, sl st in first sc on RS of Right Front, *ch 2, sl st in 2nd dc of next shell on WS of Back, sl st in 2nd dc of corresponding shell on RS of Right Front, ch 2, sl st in next sc on WS of Back, rep from * across, ch 2, sl st in last sc on RS of Right Front, fasten off.

SLEEVE
Make 2.
Row 1 (RS): Beg at cuff, ch 44 [50, 56, 56, 56, 62], sc in 2nd ch from hook, *sk next 2 chs, shell in next ch, sk next 2 chs, sc in next ch, rep from * across, turn. *(7 [8, 9, 9, 9, 10] shells)*

Row 2: Ch 5, sc in 2nd dc of next shell, *ch 5, sc in 2nd dc of next shell, rep from * across to last sc, ch 2, dc in last sc, turn. *(6 [7, 8, 8, 8, 9] ch-5 sps, 7 [8, 9, 9, 9, 10] sc, 1 dc)*

Row 3: Ch 1, sc in first st, shell in next sc, *sc in next ch-5 sp, shell in next sc, rep from * across to last st, sc in last st, turn. *(7 [8, 9, 9, 9, 10] shells, 8 [9, 10, 10, 10, 11] sc)*

Row 4: Ch 4, dc in same st, ch 2, sc in 2nd dc of next shell, *ch 5, sc in 2nd dc of next shell, rep from * across to last st, ch 2, (dc, ch 1, dc) in last st, turn. *(6 [7, 8, 8, 8, 9] ch-5 sps, 7 [8, 9, 9, 9, 10] sc, 4 dc)*

Row 5: Ch 4, dc in same st, sc in next dc, shell in next sc, *sc in next ch-5 sp, shell in next sc, rep from * across to last 2 sts, sc in next dc, (dc, ch 1, dc) in last st, turn. *(7 [8, 9, 9, 9, 10] shells, 8 [9, 10, 10, 10, 11] sc, 4 dc)*

Row 6: Ch 1, sc in first st, ch 5, *sc in 2nd dc of next shell, ch 5, rep from * across to last st, sc in last st, turn. *(8 [9, 11, 11, 11, 12] ch-5 sps, 9 [10, 12, 12, 12, 13] sc)*

Row 7: Beg shell in first st, *sc in next ch-5 sp, shell in next sc, rep from * across, turn. *(9 [10, 11, 11, 11, 12] shells, 8 [9, 10, 10, 10, 11] sc)*

Row 8: Ch 5, sc in 2nd dc of first shell, *ch 5, sc in 2nd dc of next shell, rep from * across, ch 2, dc in last st of same shell, turn. *(8 [9, 11, 11, 11, 12] ch-5 sps, 9 [10, 12, 12, 12, 13] sc, 1 dc)*

Row 9: Ch 1, sc in first st, shell in next sc, *sc in next ch-5 sp, shell in next sc, rep from * across to last st, sc in last st, turn. *(9 [10, 11, 11, 11, 12] shells, 10 [11, 12, 12, 12, 13] sc)*

Rows 10–17 [10–17, 10–17, 10–25, 10–25, 10–25]: [Rep rows 2–9 consecutively] 1 [1, 1, 2, 2, 2] time(s). *(11 [12, 13, 15, 15, 16] shells at end of last row)*

Next Rows: [Rep rows 2 and 9 alternately] 9 [10, 10, 7, 8, 8] times. Fasten off at end of last row.

ASSEMBLY
Matching center of last row on Sleeves to shoulder seams, sew Sleeves in place. Sew Sleeve and side seams.

BODY TRIM
Working around entire outer edge in ends of rows and in starting ch across bottom, join with sc in bottom right-hand corner, *sk next 2 chs, shell in next ch, sk next 2 chs, sc in next ch, rep from * across, shell in next row, **sc in next row, shell in next row, rep from ** around fronts and neck to bottom left-hand corner, join in beg sc, fasten off.

SLEEVE TRIM
Beg at seam, working in opposite side of starting ch on 1 Sleeve, join with sc in first ch, sk next 3 chs, shell in next ch, sk next 2 chs, *sc in next ch, sk next 2 chs, shell in next ch, sk next 2 chs, rep from * around, join in beg sc, fasten off.

Rep on other Sleeve. •

Shimmering Shell Skirt

Design by Jill Hanratty

SKILL LEVEL

INTERMEDIATE

FINISHED SIZES

Instructions given fit woman's X-small waist; changes for small waist, medium waist, large waist, X-large waist, 2X-large waist, 3X-large waist and 4X-large waist are in [ ].

FINISHED GARMENT MEASUREMENTS

Waist: 29 inches *(X-small)* [31½ inches *(small)*, 33¾ inches *(medium)*, 38½ inches *(large)*, 41 inches *(X-large)*, 43½ inches *(2X-large)*, 48¼ inches *(3X-large)*, 53 inches *(4X-large)*]

Hips: 36 inches *(X-small)* [38½ inches *(small)*, 40¾ inches *(medium)*, 43¼ inches *(large)*, 45½ inches *(X-large)*, 50½ inches *(2X-large)*, 55¼ inches *(3X-large)*, 60 inches *(4X-large)*]

MATERIALS

- Patons Brilliant light (light worsted) weight yarn (1¾ oz/166 yds/ 50g per ball):
    7 [8, 8, 9, 10, 11, 12, 14] balls #04913 marvelous mocha
- Size G/6/4mm crochet hook or size needed to obtain gauge
- Tapestry needle

GAUGE

6 shells and 6 sc = 6 inches; 5 rows in pattern = 2 inches

Join with a slip stitch unless otherwise stated.

Chain-3 at beginning of double crochet round counts as first double crochet unless otherwise stated.

Extended single crochet (extended sc): Insert hook in next st, yo, pull lp through, yo, pull through 1 lp on hook *(first step)*, yo, pull through 2 lps on *hook (2nd step)*.

Shell: 5 dc in indicated st.

INSTRUCTIONS

WAISTBAND

Row 1: Ch 2, **extended sc** *(see Special Stitches)* in 2nd ch from hook, [extended sc in first step of last extended sc] 144 [156, 168, 192, 204, 216, 240, 264] times, turn. *(145 [157, 169, 193, 205, 217, 241, 265] extended sc)*

Row 2: Ch 4 *(counts as first dc and ch-1 sp)*, sk next st, dc in next st, [ch 1, sk next st, dc in next st] across, turn. *(73 [79, 85, 97, 103, 109, 121, 133] dc, 72 [78, 84, 96, 102, 108, 120, 132] ch sps)*

Row 3: Ch 1, sc in each st and in each ch sp across, turn. *(145 [157, 169, 193, 205, 217, 241, 265] sc)*

SKIRT

Rnd 1: Now working in rnds, **ch 3** *(see Pattern Notes)*, 2 dc in first st, sk next 2 sts, sc in next st, sk next 2 sts, ***shell** (see Special Stitches)* in next st, sk next 2 sts, sc in next st, sk next 2 sts, rep from * across to last st, 2 dc in last st, join in 3rd ch of beg ch-3, **turn**. *(First 3 sts and last 2 sts count*

as a shell) (24 [26, 28, 32, 34, 36, 40, 44] shells, 24 [26, 28, 32, 34, 36, 40, 44] sc)

Rnd 2: Ch 1, sc in first st, shell in next sc, *sc in 3rd dc of next shell, shell in next sc, rep from * around, join in beg sc, turn.

Rnd 3: Ch 3, dc in same sc, sc in 3rd dc of next shell, *shell in next sc, sc in 3rd dc of next shell, rep from * around, 3 dc in same st as beg ch-3, join in 3rd ch of beg ch-3, turn.

Rnd 4: Ch 1, sc in first st, 3 dc in next st, sc in next st, [shell in next sc, sc in center st of next shell] 11 [12, 13, 15, 16, 17, 19, 21] times, shell in next sc, sc in 2nd dc of next shell, 3 dc in next st, sc in next st, [shell in next sc, sc in center st of next shell] 11 [12, 13, 15, 16, 17, 19, 21] times, shell in next sc, join in beg sc, turn. *(24 [26, 28, 32, 34, 36, 40, 44] shells, 25 [27, 29, 33, 35, 37, 41, 45] sc, 2 3-dc groups)*

Rnd 5: Ch 3, dc in same st, [sc in 3rd dc of next shell, shell in next sc] 11 [12, 13, 15, 16, 17, 19, 21] times, sc in 3rd dc of next shell, 3 dc in next sc, sc in 2nd dc of next 3-dc group, 3 dc in next sc, [sc in 3rd dc of next shell, shell in next sc] 11 [12, 13, 15, 16, 17, 19, 21] times, sc in 3rd dc of next shell, 3 dc in next sc, sc in 2nd dc of next 3-dc group, dc in same st as first ch-3, join in 3rd ch of beg ch-3, turn. *(22 [24, 26, 30, 32, 34, 38, 42] shells, 26 [28, 30, 34, 36, 38, 42, 46] sc, 4 3-dc groups)*

Rnd 6: Ch 1, sc in first st, shell in each sc and sc in 2nd dc of each 3-dc group and in 3rd dc of each shell around, join in beg sc. *(26 [28, 30, 34, 36, 38, 42, 46] shells, 27 [29, 31, 35, 37, 39, 43, 47] sc)*

Rnd 7: Ch 3, 2 dc in first st, sc in 3rd dc of each shell and shell in each sc

around, 2 dc in same st as beg ch-3, join in 3rd ch of beg ch-3, turn.

Rnds 8 & 9: Rep rnds 2 and 3.

Rnd 10: Ch 1, sc in first st, *3 dc in next dc, sc in next dc, [shell in next sc, sc in 3rd dc of next shell] 12 [13, 14, 16, 17, 18, 20, 22] times, shell in next sc*, sc in 2nd dc of next shell, 3 dc in next dc, sc in next dc, [shell in next sc, sc in 3rd dc of next shell] 12 [13, 14, 16, 17, 18, 20, 22] times, shell in next sc, join in beg sc, turn. *(26 [28, 30, 34, 36, 38, 42, 46] shells, 28 [30, 32, 36, 38, 40, 44, 48] sc, 2 3-dc groups)*

Rnd 11: Ch 3, dc in first st, [sc in 3rd dc of next shell, shell in next sc] 12 [13, 14, 16, 17, 18, 20, 22] times, sc in 3rd dc of next shell, 3 dc in next sc, sc in 2nd dc of next 3-dc group, 3 dc in next sc, [sc in 3rd dc of next shell, shell in next sc] 12 [13, 14, 16, 17, 18, 20, 22] times, sc in 3rd dc of next shell, 3 dc in next sc, sc in 2nd dc of next 3-dc group, dc in same st as first ch-3, join in 3rd ch of beg ch-3, turn. *(24 [26, 28, 32, 34, 36, 40, 44] shells, 4 3-dc groups, 28 [30, 32, 36, 38, 40, 44, 48] sc)*

Rnd 12: Ch 1, sc in first st, shell in each sc and sc in 2nd dc of each 3-dc group and in 3rd dc of each shell around, join in beg sc, turn. *(28 [30, 32, 36, 38, 44, 48] shells, 28 [30, 32, 36, 38, 40, 44, 48] sc)*

Rnd 13: Rep rnd 7.

Rnds 14 & 15: Rep rnds 2 and 3.

Rnd 16: Ch 1, sc in first st, 3 dc in next dc, sc in next dc, [shell in next sc, sc in 3rd dc of next shell] 13 [14, 15, 17, 18, 19, 21, 23] times, shell in next sc, sc in 2nd dc of next shell, 3 dc in next dc, sc in next dc, [shell in next sc, sc in 3rd dc of next shell] 13 [14, 15, 17, 18, 19, 21, 23] times, shell in next sc, join in beg sc, turn. *(28 [30,*

32, 36, 38, 44, 48] shells, 30 [32, 34, 38, 40, 42, 46, 50] sc, 2 3-dc groups)

Rnd 17: Ch 3, dc in same st, [sc in 3rd dc of next shell, shell in next sc] 13 [14, 15, 17, 18, 19, 21, 23] times, sc in 3rd dc of next shell, 3 dc in next sc, sc in 2nd dc of next 3-dc group, 3 dc in next sc, [sc in 3rd dc of next shell, shell in next sc] 13 [14, 15, 17, 18, 19, 21, 23] times, sc in 3rd dc of next shell, 3 dc in next sc, sc in center st of next 3-dc group, dc in same sc as beg ch-3, join in 3rd ch of beg ch-3, turn. *(26 [28, 30, 34, 36, 38, 42, 46] shells, 32 [34, 36, 40, 42, 44, 48, 52] sc, 4 3-dc groups)*

Rnd 18: Ch 1, sc in first st, shell in each sc and sc in 2nd dc of each 3-dc group and in 3rd dc of each shell around, join in beg sc, turn. *(30 [32, 34, 38, 40, 42, 46, 50] shells)*

Rnd 19: Rep rnd 7.

Next rnds: [Rep rnds 2 and 3 alternately] 16 [16, 17, 17, 18, 18, 19, 19] times or to desired length.

TRIM

Rnd 1: Ch 1, sc in first st, *ch 5, sc in 3rd dc of next shell, rep from * around, join in beg ch-1, dc in first sc. *(30 [32, 34, 38, 40, 42, 46, 50] ch sps)*

Rnd 2: Ch 1, sc in sp formed by joining dc, 7 dc in next sc, *sc in 3rd ch of next ch-5 sp, 7 dc in next sc, rep from * around, join in beg sc.

Rnd 3: Ch 3, 6 dc in same st, ch 5, *7 dc in next sc, ch 5, rep from * around, join in 3rd ch of beg ch-3, fasten off.

DRAWSTRING

With 2 strands held tog, ch 160 [180, 200, 230, 250 280, 300, 330], fasten off.

FINISHING

Weave Drawstring through ch sps of row 2 on Waistband. ●

Single Simple Skirt

Design by Jill Hanratty

SKILL LEVEL

EASY

FINISHED SIZES

Instructions given fit woman's X-small waist; changes for small waist, medium waist, large waist, X-large waist, 2X-large waist, 3X-large waist and 4X-large waist are in [ ].

FINISHED GARMENT MEASUREMENTS

Waist: 32 inches *(X-small)* [34 inches *(small)*, 36 inches *(medium)*, 38 inches *(large)*, 42 inches *(X-large)*, 46 inches *(2X-large)*, 50 inches *(3X-large)*, 54 inches *(4X-large)*]

Hips: 38 inches *(X-small)* [40 inches *(small)*, 42 inches *(medium)*, 44 inches *(large)*, 48 inches *(X-large)*, 52 inches *(2X-large)*, 56 inches *(3X-large)*, 60 inches *(4X-large)*]

MATERIALS

- Lion Brand Babysoft light (light worsted) weight yarn (5 oz/459 yds/140g per ball):
  3 [3, 3, 4, 4, 5, 5, 5] balls #111 navy
- Size I/9/5.5mm crochet hook or size needed to obtain gauge

GAUGE

4 extended sc = 1 inch; 5 rows = 2 inches

PATTERN NOTE

Join with a slip stitch unless otherwise stated.

Extended single crochet (extended sc): Insert hook in next st, yo, pull lp through, yo, pull through 1 lp on hook *(first step)*, yo, pull through 2 lps on hook *(2nd step)*.

INSTRUCTIONS

WAISTBAND

Row 1: Ch 2, **extended sc** *(see Special Stitch)* in 2nd ch from hook, [extended sc in first step of last extended sc] 127 [135, 143, 151, 167, 183, 199, 215] times, turn. *(128 [136, 144, 152, 168, 184, 200, 216] extended sc)*

Row 2 (RS): Ch 3 *(counts as first dc)*, dc in next st, [ch 1, sk next st, dc in next st] across, turn. *(65 [69, 73, 77, 85, 93, 101, 109] dc, 63 [67, 71, 75, 83, 91, 99, 107] ch sps)*

SKIRT

Rnd 1: Now working in rnds, ch 1, sc in each st and in each ch sp around, join in beg sc, **turn**. *(128 [136, 144, 152, 168, 184, 200, 216] sc)*

Rnd 2: Ch 1, extended sc in first st, ch 1, sk next st, [extended sc in next st, ch 1, sk next st] twice, (extended sc, ch 1) twice in next st, sk next st, *[extended sc in next st, ch 1, sk next st] 3 times, (extended sc, ch 1) twice in next st, sk next st, rep from * around, join with sc in beg extended sc, turn. *(80 [85, 90, 95, 105, 115, 125, 135] extended sc, 80 [85, 90, 95, 105, 115, 125, 135] ch sps)*

Rnds 3–8: Ch 1, extended sc in first st, ch 1, sk next ch sp, *extended sc in next st, ch 1, sk next st, rep from * around, join in beg sc.

Rnd 9: Ch 1, extended sc in first st, ch 1, sk next st, [extended sc in next st, ch 1, sk next st] 14 [15, 16, 17, 19, 21, 23, 25] times, [extended sc, ch 1] twice in next st, sk next st, *[extended sc in next st, ch 1, sk next st] 15 [16, 17, 18, 20, 22, 24, 26] times, [extended sc, ch 1] twice in next st, sk next st, rep from * around, join in beg sc, turn. *(85 [90, 95, 100, 110, 120, 130, 140] extended sc, 85 [90, 95, 100, 110, 120, 130, 140] ch sps)*

Rnds 10–13: Rep rnd 3.

Rnd 14: Ch 1, extended sc in first st, ch 1, sk next st, [extended sc in next st, ch 1, sk next st] 15 [16, 17, 18, 29, 22, 24, 26] times, [extended sc, ch 1] twice in next st, *[extended sc in next st, ch 1, sk next st] 16 [17, 18, 19, 21, 23, 25, 27] times, [extended sc, ch 1] twice in next st, rep from * around, join in beg sc, turn. *(90 [95, 100, 105, 115, 125, 135, 145] extended sc, 90 [95, 100, 105, 115, 125, 135, 145] ch sps)*

Rnds 15–18: Rep rnd 3.

Rnd 19: Ch 1, extended sc in first st, ch 1, sk next st, [extended sc in next st, ch 1, sk next st] 16 [17, 18, 19, 21, 23, 25, 27] times, [extended sc, ch 1] twice in next st, *[extended sc in next st, ch 1, sk next st] 17 [18, 19, 20, 22, 24, 26, 28] times, [extended sc, ch 1] twice in next st, rep from * around, join in beg sc, turn. *(95 [100, 105, 110, 120, 130, 140, 150] extended sc, (95 [100, 105, 110, 120, 130, 140, 150] ch sps)*

Next rnds: [Rep rnd 3] 37 [37, 39, 39, 41, 41, 43, 43] times or until Skirt reaches desired length. Fasten off at end of last rnd.

DRAWSTRING

With 2 strands held tog, ch 160 [180, 200, 230, 250, 280, 300, 330], fasten off.

FINISHING

Weave Drawstring through ch sps of row 2 of Waistband. •

Evening Elegance Skirt

Design by Jill Hanratty

SKILL LEVEL

EASY

FINISHED SIZES

Instructions given fit woman's X-small waist; changes for small waist, medium waist, large waist, X-large waist, 2X-large waist, 3X-large waist and 4X-large waist are in [ ].

FINISHED GARMENT MEASUREMENTS

Waist: 32 inches *(X-small)* [34 inches *(small)*, 36 inches *(medium)*, 38 inches *(large)*, 42 inches *(X-large)*, 46 inches *(2X-large)*, 50 inches *(3X-large)*, 54 inches *(4X-large)*]

Hips: 36 inches *(X-small)* [38 inches *(small)*, 40 inches *(medium)*, 42 inches *(large)*, 46 inches *(X-large)*, 50 inches *(2X-large)*, 54 inches *(3X-large)*, 58 inches *(4X-large)*]

MATERIALS

- Patons Brilliant light (light worsted) weight yarn (1¾ oz/166 yds/ 50g per ball):
  7 [7, 8, 9, 10, 11, 12, 13, 14] balls #04940 black dazzle
- Size H/8/5mm crochet hook or size need to obtain gauge

GAUGE

4 sts = 1 inch; 7 rows in pattern = 2 inches

PATTERN NOTE

Join with a slip stitch unless otherwise stated.

Extended single crochet (extended sc): Insert hook in next st, yo, pull lp through, yo, pull through 1 lp on hook *(first step)*, yo, pull through 2 lps on hook *(2nd step)*.

INSTRUCTIONS

WAISTBAND

Row 1: Ch 2, **extended sc** *(see Special Stitch)* in 2nd ch from hook, [extended sc in first step of last extended sc] 127 [135, 143, 151, 167, 183, 199, 215] times, turn. *(128 [136, 144, 152, 168, 184, 200, 216] extended sc)*

Row 2 (RS): Ch 3 *(counts as first dc)*, dc in next st, [ch 1, sk next st, dc in next st] across, turn. *(65 [69, 73, 77, 85, 93, 101, 109] dc, 63 [67, 71, 75, 83, 91, 99, 107] ch sps)*

SKIRT

Rnd 3: Now working in rnds, ch 1, sc in first st, dc in next ch sp, [sc in next st or ch sp, dc in next st or ch sp] around, join in beg sc, **turn**. *(128 [136, 144, 152, 168, 184, 200, 216] sts)*

Rnds 4–13 [4–13, 4–14, 4–14, 4–15, 4–15, 4–16, 4–16]: Ch 1, sc in same st, dc in next st, [sc in next st, dc in next st] around, join in beg sc.

Rnd 14 [14, 15, 15, 16, 16, 17, 17]: Ch 1, sc in same st, dc in next st, [sc in next st, dc in next st] 14 [15, 16, 17, 19, 21, 23, 25] times, (sc, dc) in each of next 2 sts, *[sc in next st, dc in next st] 15 [16, 17, 18, 20, 22, 24, 26] times, (sc, dc) in each of next 2 sts, rep from * around, join in beg sc. *(136 [144, 152, 160, 176, 192, 208, 224] sts)*

Rnds 15–23 [15–23, 16–24, 16–24, 17–26, 17–26, 18–28, 18–28]: Rep rnd 4.

Rnd 24 [24, 25, 25, 27, 27, 29, 29]: Ch 1, sc in same st, dc in next st, [sc in next st, dc in next st] 15 [16, 17, 18, 20, 22, 24, 26] times, (sc, dc) in each of next 2 sts, *[sc in next st, dc in next st] 16 [17, 18, 19, 21, 23, 25, 27] times, (sc, dc) in each of next 2 sts, rep from * around, join in beg sc. *(144 [152, 160, 168, 184, 200, 216, 232] sts)*

Next rnds: [Rep rnd 4] 52 [54, 55, 57, 57, 57, 57, 59] times or to desired length less ½ inch.

TRIM

Rnd 1: Ch 1, sc in same st, ch 4, sk next 3 sts, [sc in next st, ch 5, sk next 3 sts] around, join in beg sc, **turn**. *(36 [38, 40, 42, 46, 50, 54, 58] ch sps)*

Rnd 2: Ch 1, 5 sc in each ch sp around, join in beg sc, fasten off.

DRAWSTRING

With 2 strands held tog, ch 160 [180, 200, 230, 250, 280, 300, 330], fasten off.

FINISHING

Weave Drawstring through ch sps of row 2 of Waistband. •

TOLL-FREE ORDER LINE or to request a free catalog (800) LV-ANNIE (800) 582-6643
Customer Service (800) AT-ANNIE (800) 282-6643, **Fax** (800) 882-6643
Visit anniesattic.com

We have made every effort to ensure the accuracy and completeness of these instructions.
We cannot, however, be responsible for human error, typographical mistakes or variations in individual work.

ISBN: 978-1-59635-186-8

Printed in USA   1 2 3 4 5 6 7 8 9

Stitch Guide

ABBREVIATIONS

beg	begin/beginning
bpdc	back post double crochet
bpsc	back post single crochet
bptr	back post treble crochet
CC	contrasting color
ch	chain stitch
ch-	refers to chain or space previously made (i.e., ch-1 space)
ch sp	chain space
cl	cluster
cm	centimeter(s)
dc	double crochet
dec	decrease/decreases/decreasing
dtr	double treble crochet
fpdc	front post double crochet
fpsc	front post single crochet
fptr	front post treble crochet
g	gram(s)
hdc	half double crochet
inc	increase/increases/increasing
lp(s)	loop(s)
MC	main color
mm	millimeter(s)
oz	ounce(s)
pc	popcorn
rem	remain/remaining
rep	repeat(s)
rnd(s)	round(s)
RS	right side
sc	single crochet
sk	skip(ped)
sl st	slip stitch
sp(s)	space(s)
st(s)	stitch(es)
tog	together
tr	treble crochet
trtr	triple treble
WS	wrong side
yd(s)	yard(s)
yo	yarn over

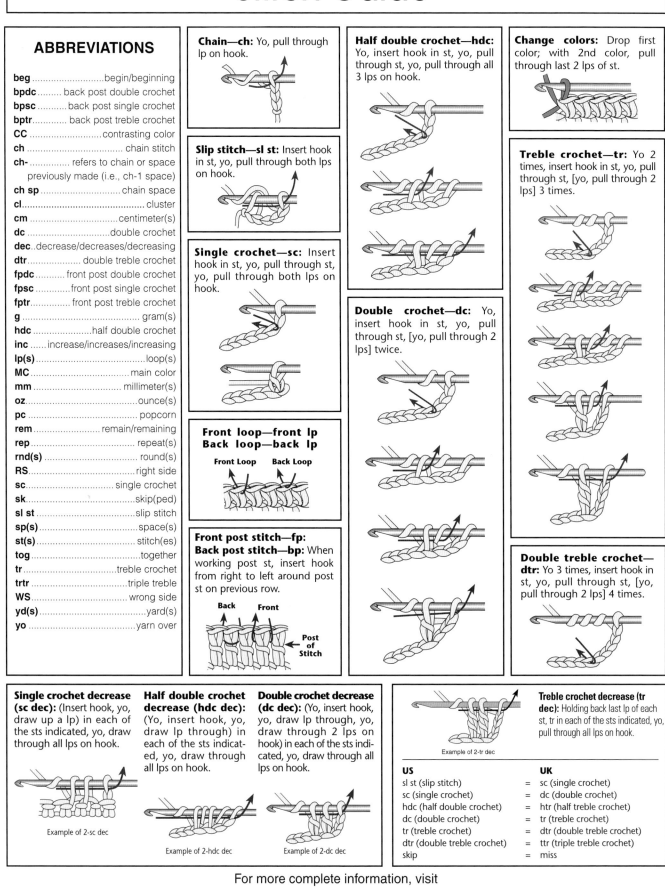

Chain—ch: Yo, pull through lp on hook.

Slip stitch—sl st: Insert hook in st, yo, pull through both lps on hook.

Single crochet—sc: Insert hook in st, yo, pull through st, yo, pull through both lps on hook.

**Front loop—front lp
Back loop—back lp**

Front Loop   Back Loop

**Front post stitch—fp:
Back post stitch—bp:** When working post st, insert hook from right to left around post st on previous row.

Back   Front

Post of Stitch

Half double crochet—hdc: Yo, insert hook in st, yo, pull through st, yo, pull through all 3 lps on hook.

Double crochet—dc: Yo, insert hook in st, yo, pull through st, [yo, pull through 2 lps] twice.

Change colors: Drop first color; with 2nd color, pull through last 2 lps of st.

Treble crochet—tr: Yo 2 times, insert hook in st, yo, pull through st, [yo, pull through 2 lps] 3 times.

Double treble crochet—dtr: Yo 3 times, insert hook in st, yo, pull through st, [yo, pull through 2 lps] 4 times.

Single crochet decrease (sc dec): (Insert hook, yo, draw up a lp) in each of the sts indicated, yo, draw through all lps on hook.

Example of 2-sc dec

Half double crochet decrease (hdc dec): (Yo, insert hook, yo, draw lp through) in each of the sts indicated, yo, draw through all lps on hook.

Example of 2-hdc dec

Double crochet decrease (dc dec): (Yo, insert hook, yo, draw lp through, yo, draw through 2 lps on hook) in each of the sts indicated, yo, draw through all lps on hook.

Example of 2-dc dec

Treble crochet decrease (tr dec): Holding back last lp of each st, tr in each of the sts indicated, yo, pull through all lps on hook.

Example of 2-tr dec

US	UK
sl st (slip stitch)	= sc (single crochet)
sc (single crochet)	= dc (double crochet)
hdc (half double crochet)	= htr (half treble crochet)
dc (double crochet)	= tr (treble crochet)
tr (treble crochet)	= dtr (double treble crochet)
dtr (double treble crochet)	= ttr (triple treble crochet)
skip	= miss

For more complete information, visit

AnniesAttic.com